First World War
and Army of Occupation
War Diary
France, Belgium and Germany

27 DIVISION
Divisional Troops
Royal Army Medical Corps
81 Field Ambulance
22 December 1914 - 31 October 1915

WO95/2259/1

The Naval & Military Press Ltd
www.nmarchive.com
Published in association with The National Archives

Published by

The Naval & Military Press Ltd

Unit 10 Ridgewood Industrial Park,
Uckfield, East Sussex,
TN22 5QE England
Tel: +44 (0) 1825 749494

www.naval-military-press.com
www.nmarchive.com

This diary has been reprinted in facsimile from the original. Any imperfections are inevitably reproduced and the quality may fall short of modern type and cartographic standards.

© Crown Copyright
Images reproduced by permission of The National Archives, London, England, 2015.

Contents

Document type	Place/Title	Date From	Date To
Heading	WO95/2259/1		
Heading	27th Division Medical 81st Field Ambulance Dec 1914-Oct 1915		
Heading	81st Field Ambulance (27th Division) Vol I		
War Diary	Havre	22/12/1914	23/12/1914
War Diary	Aire	25/12/1914	31/12/1914
Heading	No 81 Field Ambulance Vol I 27 Division		
War Diary	Aire	05/01/1915	05/01/1915
War Diary	Borre	06/01/1915	06/01/1915
War Diary	Ouderdom	08/01/1915	16/01/1915
War Diary	Dickebusch	27/01/1915	31/01/1915
Heading	81st Field Ambulance 27th Division Vol II		
War Diary	Dickebusch	28/02/1915	28/02/1915
Heading	81st Field Ambulance, 27th Division Expeditionary Force 121/5256 War Diary Of Lt. Col. J.M. Rogers-Tills Tone Commanding 81st Field Ambulance, R.A.M.C. From March 1st 1915 To March 31st 1915 (Volume III)		
War Diary	Dickebusch	02/03/1915	02/03/1915
War Diary	Reninghelst	10/03/1915	31/03/1915
Heading	81st Field Ambulance, 27th Division, Expeditionary Force 121/5256 War Diary Of Lt. Col. J.M. Rogers Tills Tone Comdg. 81st Field Ambulance, R.A.M.C. From April 1st 1915 To April 30th 1915 (Volume IV)		
War Diary	Ypres	01/04/1915	20/04/1915
War Diary	Poperinghe	22/04/1915	30/04/1915
Heading	27th Division 81st Field Ambulance Vol V May		
War Diary	Poperinghe	01/05/1915	31/05/1915
Heading	27th Division 81st Field Ambulance Vol VI June 15		
War Diary		01/06/1915	30/06/1915
Heading	27th Division 81st Field Ambulance Vol VII July 15		
War Diary		03/07/1915	30/07/1915
Miscellaneous	Statement Of Particulars Of No. RAAG Rank & Amt		
Heading	27th Division 81st Field Ambulance Vol VIII August 15		
War Diary		03/08/1915	29/08/1915
Heading	27th Division 81st Field Ambulance Vol IX Sept 15		
War Diary		01/09/1915	30/09/1915
Heading	27th Division 81st Fd Ambulance Oct-15 Vol X		
War Diary	Morcourt	02/10/1915	04/10/1915
Map	Illustrating Gearance Of 81st Brigade		
War Diary		04/10/1915	04/10/1915
War Diary	Morcourt	05/10/1915	27/10/1915
War Diary	Bougainville	28/10/1915	31/10/1915

WO95/2259/1

27TH DIVISION
MEDICAL

81ST FIELD AMBULANCE

DEC 1914 - OCT 1915

12/4/665.

81st Field Ambulance (24th Division)

Vol I.

Dec '14
Oct '15

12/4/665
Dec 1914

Dec/14

WAR DIARY
or
INTELLIGENCE SUMMARY.
(Erase heading not required.)

Army Form C. 2118.

Hour, Date, Place	Summary of Events and Information	Remarks and references to Appendices
1914 Dec 22nd HAVRE	arrived at the port early morning, stood off for some hours, part of the Transport disembarked about 10.15 pm.	
" 23rd	Marched from the Docks 10.30 last night, arrived at No. 2 Rest Camp about 2 o'clock this morning.	
" 25th AIRE	Marched out of rest camp & reached HAVRE Maritime Station 12 noon yesterday, entrained, train moved at 4.30 pm, reached AIRE 4.30 this afternoon. The watering of horses on the journey would have been simplified had the length of the halts been noticed; also this would have been easier for returning j nature to the journey however. Horses watered on completion in 1½ hours, & detraining was completed out of AIRE station at START time, & billets at MOUZIN LE COMTE, on outskirts of the town.	

WAR DIARY
or
INTELLIGENCE SUMMARY.
(Erase heading not required.)

Army Form C. 2118.

Instructions regarding War Diaries and Intelligence Summaries are contained in F.S. Regs., Part II. and the Staff Manual respectively. Title pages will be prepared in manuscript.

Hour, Date, Place	Summary of Events and Information	Remarks and references to Appendices
10/14		
Dec 25 continued AIRE	Orders received detailing the Units to the 31st & 2/5 Bgde. quartered in the town.	
Dec 26 "	Established a reception ward for casual sick of the Bgde. who cannot be treated regimentally. There are the vacancies & S. Omer. The Motor ambulances to complete establishment joined the Unit this day.	
	Car to vacate to S. OMER with my own motor transport	
Dec 31 "	Numbers evacuated have not been large; mostly sore feet from want of cleanliness and a few cases of influenza. Visited the Units and witnessed in the Regt. Med. Officers the necessity of their informing their CO the importance of frequent foot inspections	

No. 81 Field Ambulance.

Vol I
27 Division

WAR DIARY
or
INTELLIGENCE SUMMARY.
(Erase heading not required.)

Army Form C. 2118.

Instructions regarding War Diaries and Intelligence Summaries are contained in F.S. Regs., Part II. and the Staff Manual respectively. Title pages will be prepared in manuscript.

Hour, Date, Place	Summary of Events and Information	Remarks and references to Appendices
1915 Jan 5th AIRE	Orders received to march out of AIRE at 9.30 a.m. tomorrow to BORRÉ. Nothing to note with respect to residence of Command. Quiet night at AIRE.	
Jan 6th BORRÉ	Arrived at dusk. Orders received to march out at 8.30 a.m. and proceed to DICKEBUSCH, avoiding road via LA CLYTTE.	
Jan 8th OUDERDOM	Stopped by S. Pagtar at OUDERDOM and dismounted to billet at 7am, just outside the village, this billeting was reached at 9 p.m. last evening. Tried to find suitable building for reception of sick but failed, as this village is in the French area & all available accommodation is taken by French troops who have a field hospital here. Acting on instructions from A.D.M.S. I sent 1 officer, 10 N.C.O's, rank and file, with motor ambulance to staff a collecting & evening station at WESTOUTRE— and the rest of my ground cycle of battalion billeted in tents.	
Jan 16 "		

WAR DIARY or INTELLIGENCE SUMMARY

Army Form C. 2118.

Hour, Date, Place	Summary of Events and Information	Remarks and references to Appendices
16/15 Jan 27th DICKEBUSCH	Relieved 83rd Field Ambulance in front area at DICKEBUSCH, having with drawn the party from WESTOUTRE. Have this party being relieved by a party from the 83rd Field Ambulance. The billeting & Bearing Station. During the 10 days admitted and transferred 212 cases, mostly "foot" cases, and some frost-bite. The Dressing Station at DICKEBUSCH comprises 3 large rooms, kitchen & small room for Office, with a sufficiently large lath-&-straw; No 1 the 3 large rooms has a tiled floor & I have had this converted into 3 surgeries by means of wire stretchers across, & good sheets as curtains. The this the large room will accommodate 68 lying down cases. These lofts will accommodate 9 men with stores with blankets and room are heated. For sitting cases & some Accommodation for 70 additional lying down cases is found in a milk sterilising building near by.	[signature]

Army Form C. 2118.

WAR DIARY
or
INTELLIGENCE SUMMARY.
(Erase heading not required.)

Hour, Date, Place	Summary of Events and Information	Remarks and references to Appendices

1915

Jan 31. DICKEBUSCH

From midday Jan. 27th 305 cases have passed through the Field Ambulance — 77 wounded, comprising — Bullet 40, Shell 35; the majority of the balance being more severe "frost feet", & some sprinkling of dysentery & colitis. Some 400 slight cases have been evacuated to BOESCHEPE for retention by 82nd Field Ambulance. The great majority of these are slightly "frost-footed", the general cases of simple trouble here detained, & several cases of simple trouble & retained at their units.

The majority of bullet exit wounds were numerous in size, and would suggest expanding bullets, but probably the bullets got "head side on" in their experience resistance, as the base of the bullets having more substance would have greater momentum than the slighter point. In no case of bullets hand [?] the slightest... there was a smell refused [?]

Army Form C. 2118.

WAR DIARY
or
INTELLIGENCE SUMMARY.
(Erase heading not required.)

Instructions regarding War Diaries and Intelligence Summaries are contained in F.S. Regs., Part II. and the Staff Manual respectively. Title pages will be prepared in manuscript.

Hour, Date, Place	Summary of Events and Information	Remarks and references to Appendices

Work in front & but at the back of the shelters was a serious job though which the whole of the head of the trenches had been carried completely away.

Organisation of Field Ambulance. The 3 section organisation did not appear to be well suited to obtain the maximum of work in this siege warfare. Therefore I divided the unit into 4 H.Qrs. and 2 half ambulances, half working 24 hours & half resting. This organisation was worked admirably, giving 2 med Officers for duty at the Dressing Station, and 2 Med Officers with the bearer subdivision; the bearer subdivision of each half ambulance being subdivided into 2 subsections.

Probably during action the new 3 section organization will prove the better.

(9 20 6) W 4141—463 100,000 9/14 H W V Forms/C. 2118/10

121/4665

121/4665
Decr. 1915

81st Field Ambulance — 24th Division

Vol II

AMD

WAR DIARY
or
INTELLIGENCE SUMMARY.
(Erase heading not required.)

Army Form C. 2118.

Hour, Date, Place	Summary of Events and Information	Remarks and references to Appendices
1915 Feb. 28th DICKEBUSCH	There has been nothing of specially note during the month. The field ambulance has remained in the front area. During the 28 days 1572 cases have passed through the field ambulance of which 597 have been sick; These comprise Bullet 439; Shell 97; Grenade 7; Bayonet 4. Most of the balance were "frost" feet & some dysentery. In addition to the above, some 1500 have been sent to the composite battalion at BOESCHEPE most of whom were slow marked minor trench troubles & "frost" feet of lower degree. The cases of "frost" feet show marked diminution towards the end of the month. Over & above the foregoing, many cases here detained for treatment for simple diarrhoea & were returned to their units. The weather from the beginning of Feb 1915 to the end worked smoothly at all times, and	

Army Form C. 2118.

WAR DIARY
or
INTELLIGENCE SUMMARY.
(Erase heading not required.)

Instructions regarding War Diaries and Intelligence Summaries are contained in F. S. Regs., Part II. and the Staff Manual respectively. Title pages will be prepared in manuscript.

Hour, Date, Place	Summary of Events and Information	Remarks and references to Appendices
	We have ambulances forward investigate on very 2nd nights, so there can be got on to the road again after getting off, which is not the case with another ambulance. Motor ambulances are the more useful on light nights, when the edge of the road can be seen.	

Confidential

81st FIELD AMBULANCE,
27th DIVISION.
EXPEDITIONARY FORCE.

121/5256

WAR DIARY
of
Lt. Col. J. M. Rogers-Tillstone
Commanding 81st Field Ambulance,
R.A.M.C.

from March 1st 1915   to March 31st 1915

(VOLUME ~~III~~ IV)

121/5256/9/15
March 15

WAR DIARY
or
INTELLIGENCE SUMMARY.
(Erase heading not required.)

Army Form C. 2118.

Hour, Date, Place	Summary of Events and Information	Remarks and references to Appendices
1915 March 2nd DICKEBUSCH	Two wooden huts 20 x 40 ft have been completed close to the Dressing station, for the reception of patients, to increase the accommodation, each with a partition at one end, forming a small ward 10 x 20, one for women & one for men & the other for men too poorly to send to the Evacuation, these additions greatly enhance the utility of the Dressing Station, & more much required.	[stamp]
March 10th RENINGHELST	The Unit moved back to the Reserve Brigade area at RENINGHELST Today, having been relieved at DICKEBUSCH by the 83rd Field Ambulance; a party remaining 10th for 110 Mtr route & 2 motor ambulances was sent to WESTOUTRE to take over the Bleaching & Dressing Station there. Two Officers were sent to act as Regl. Med. Officers to two of the Battalions at BUSSCHEPE, & Major PEYTON was left at DICKEBUSCH when he is in Sanitary Officer for the area. The remainder of Officers I have placed in the Bleaching & Dressing Station here.	

WAR DIARY or INTELLIGENCE SUMMARY.

During these 10 days from March 1st inclusive 570 cases passed through the Field Ambulance, of which 273 were wounded. Bullet 228; Shell 29; Grenade 14; Bayonet 2.

Six weeks duty in the Front Area have been performed, and in this period 2377 cases were admitted, these included 945 wounded, made up as follows: Bullet 757
　　　　　　　　　　　　　　　　　　　　　Shell   161
　　　　　　　　　　　　　　　　　　　　　Grenade   21
　　　　　　　　　　　　　　　　　　　　　Bayonet   6

In addition to the above, over 200 cases had been transferred to the Reposito Battalion at BOESCHEPE, and several cases of simple diarrhoea were detained, treated, and sent back to their respective units.

Army Form C. 2118.

WAR DIARY
or
INTELLIGENCE SUMMARY.
(Erase heading not required.)

Instructions regarding War Diaries and Intelligence Summaries are contained in F.S. Regs., Part II. and the Staff Manual respectively. Title pages will be prepared in manuscript.

Hour, Date, Place	Summary of Events and Information	Remarks and references to Appendices
RENINGHELST March 28th	Went to YPRES with D.A.D.M.S. to look for buildings suitable for a Dressing Station & billets for the Unit and fixed up the ECOLE EPISCOPALE, a cleared place for the purpose with two large capable of holding 200 patients. Big room for 100 for surgeries, Officers ward, large court yard suitable to accommodate all the transport; the WNW angle to accommodate Operating. The square building was the nearest to and 1 ft. square building was the nearest to but for 6 beds and the rest including gate house have at my disposal. The building was meant on the strand would not billet their troops in so exposed a portion of the town.	[signatures]
RENINGHELST March 31st	Moved to proceed to above billets on the morrow, and to prepare the billeting to report April 8 no. 1. The troops at RENINGHELST and WESTOUTRE are note in ordinary coined sick sent in by Reg. M. Offrs and were kept the sickness not long been — the division.	[signatures]

Confidential.

81st FIELD AMBULANCE,
27th DIVISION,
EXPEDITIONARY FORCE.

121/5256

WAR DIARY
of
Lt. Col. J. M. Rogers-Tillstone
Cmdg. 81st Field Ambulance.
R.A.M.C.

from April 1st 1915   to April 30th 1915

(VOLUME IV)

Box 2259

Army Form C. 2118.

WAR DIARY
or
INTELLIGENCE SUMMARY.
(Erase heading not required.)

Instructions regarding War Diaries and Intelligence Summaries are contained in F. S. Regs., Part II. and the Staff Manual respectively. Title pages will be prepared in manuscript.

Hour, Date, Place	Summary of Events and Information	Remarks and references to Appendices

YPRES
April 1st
10/15

Joined the Dressing Stations at RENINGHELST and WESTOUTRE and then proceeded to ECOLE EPISCOPALE, YPRES. moved onto to ECOLE EPISCOPALE, YPRES, first arriving there at 2 P.M. the Halls were cleaned & prepared the reception being D.... A team west of the town was found for the wounded & might have like that, and my towards fighters & no fair d'angle for water cart was kept in the courtyard of the building. Half the horse division was sent out to bring in wounded from the Regt Aid-post on the ... road. The front is excellent but Aug. & the road is habitual shelled. I decided that the motor ambulances would do the work here better than horse ambulances until I had used about to extend at QUEKENBUSCH, and the 7 motor ambulances here sent ...

April 2nd

WAR DIARY
or
INTELLIGENCE SUMMARY.
(Erase heading not required.)

Army Form C. 2118.

Hour, Date, Place	Summary of Events and Information	Remarks and references to Appendices
1915 April 3rd	The Regtl Aid-post having been found very scattered, it appeared to me unnecessary so, I went with DAD.M.S. to survey the front line with a view to selecting 3 or more sites where the Regimental Aid could emerge, & do reduce the number of aid-posts, and cellars at HOOGE & dug-outs in GLENCORSE Wood & SANCTUARY Wood were selected, together with WEST-HOEK. [signature]	
April 4th	This evening 16 large shells in Hazebrouck (?) passed over this Dressing Station. [signature]	
April 5th	No-did hight in eight average 26. nought nine Hun at DICKEBUSCH. [signature] This day an x-ray was made between the plates of the travelling general used as a table for the infantry and the gutta-percha used as top, & the gutta here was used as a holder for the infantry. [signature]	

Army Form C. 2118.

WAR DIARY
or
INTELLIGENCE SUMMARY.
(Erase heading not required.)

Instructions regarding War Diaries and Intelligence Summaries are contained in F. S. Regs., Part II. and the Staff Manual respectively. Title pages will be prepared in manuscript.

Hour, Date, Place	Summary of Events and Information	Remarks and references to Appendices
1915 YPRES April 6th	The town was again shelled, and the Bulls received by 6th Bn. Sets now hit. [signed]	
April 7th	Again went over ground our site DADDLES, &c. Visited some of the Regt. Aid posts. I selected a site in SANCTUARY WOOD to erect of a log-hut on a common elaborate that should house for that part of the group coder for men, if hospital at a fixed hour — the men, if it should be taken care of by bearers. [signed]	
April 09 17 " 18th " 19th	Town again shelled, both damage [signed] " " " " " " " " Last night, one of my bearers, No. 2029 Pte R. Chapman received a bullet wound; it entered on the right side below & came out about the spleen. Having the top edge of the liver, he seems comfortable. there are as yet I need to and Kilommochzugt Station.	

Forms/C. 2118/10

Army Form C. 2118.

WAR DIARY
or
INTELLIGENCE SUMMARY.
(Erase heading not required.)

Instructions regarding War Diaries and Intelligence Summaries are contained in F.S. Regs., Part II. and the Staff Manual respectively. Title pages will be prepared in manuscript.

Hour, Date, Place	Summary of Events and Information	Remarks and references to Appendices
YPRES April 19th 1915	This morning a shell between the gatehouse that I had given up to Deborah to the Infantry, about 30 Jocatius was killed & some were hurt. The Poititgelin killed here also shelled, with about 20 casualties resulting, all the wounded received prompt attention. I caused it now to evacuate the buildings, and but all sick & wounded removed to the casemates in the rampart, and also billetted my men in some place.	
April 20th	The tom was shelled this morning by 8" and 17" incl. shells; the 17" incl. shell struck the opposite of A.D.V.S. Q.R.D.V.S. with the Grande Place and A.D.V.S. was killed. Some of my bearers proceeded to the spot and succeeded in extricating one wounded [?]. The Belgian A large number of casualties were brought in throughout the day as a result of the shelling, including the Belgian Soeurs & 3 civilians, all received attention [signed]	

WAR DIARY
or
INTELLIGENCE SUMMARY.
(Erase heading not required.)

Army Form C. 2118.

Instructions regarding War Diaries and Intelligence Summaries are contained in F.S. Regs., Part II. and the Staff Manual respectively. Title pages will be prepared in manuscript.

Hour, Date, Place	Summary of Events and Information	Remarks and references to Appendices

YPRES.
April 20th & 21st

The Ambulance was moved to home out of the town to billets at a farm with midway between BRIELEN and NOORDHOFWYK, leaving the Ambulance at the Casemates in the Ramparts; I had the motor ambulances parked in an orchard, just outside the farm, together with our water cart. I choose to hand it. I sent the resting half-advance to the new billets intact - the town is seriously unsafe to be lived in.

POPERINGHE.
April 22nd

On July at 3.30 p.m. all being quiet, no shell a sort, whilst I went out to POPERINGHE. I went out the officers to POPERINGHE to procure & that the Rest Patrol to see Lt. Holmes, one of my four sick officers, how progressing, on my return journey from POPERINGHE on the ELVERDINGHE road towards ETHELE at the cutting into the trees, troubles who I afterward be unable proceed let us

WAR DIARY
or
INTELLIGENCE SUMMARY.

Army Form C. 2118.

Hour, Date, Place	Summary of Events and Information	Remarks and references to Appendices

On account of the information that Head Quarters of Regiment proceeding towards POPERINGHE and I therefore ordered the motor ambulance to turn & proceed to the billets by way of the main YPRES road, but I found a civilian & spoke & through him some of the men who told him that their billets were being shelled, & at 11.7, as a consequence they had been ordered to place but awaits at POPERINGHE & I therefore returned to POPERINGHE, number [illegible] the wounded and one to the men and reported at Office of D.D.M.S. T. Corps, his A.D.M.S., where he told the him he knight at ELBE farm, where the 83rd Field Ambulance were billeted, this was Jan.

[signature]

Army Form C. 2118.

WAR DIARY
or
INTELLIGENCE SUMMARY.
(Erase heading not required.)

Instructions regarding War Diaries and Intelligence Summaries are contained in F.S. Regs., Part II. and the Staff Manual respectively. Title pages will be prepared in manuscript.

Hour, Date, Place	Summary of Events and Information	Remarks and references to Appendices
POPERINGHE April 23rd	Received orders to call in the Party left at YPRES and to proceed to our recopied at 82d Field Ambulance between POPERINGHE and VLAMERTINGHE, and to arrange to evacuate Regimental Aid Posts in turn with the two Field Ambulances. The above was were carried out. Lieut. C.W. Greene was detached for duty at Brit. HQrs. at POTIJZE. The party joining from YPRES informed me that the ECOLE EPISCOPALE which we had occupied in YPRES had been shelled & was in flames.	
April 30th	The mighty evacuation of the wounded have been effected in turn by the 3 field ambulances. The 82d field ambulance on night of 2 tried and I wondered if any of them tried of how to leave after leaving the hospital in	

21/7052

27/5/15 wains

81st Field Ambulance
for V
Sept 15   May.

Sept 15
May 1915
S

WAR DIARY or INTELLIGENCE SUMMARY.

81ST FIELD AMBULANCE, 27TH DIVISION, EXPEDITIONARY FORCE.

Army Form C. 2118.

(Erase heading not required.)

Hour, Date, Place	Summary of Events and Information	Remarks and references to Appendices
1915 POPERINGHE May 1st	Map. Belgium Sheet 28. 1:40,000. In compliance with orders received late last night the Ambulance proceeded from the Farm G.11.a.3.3 to Farm G.15.c.7.9. at 9 am. To billets & await orders. Qrs to MR-T	
May 2nd	Bearers collected wounded for our Div front. Qrs to MR-T	
May 3rd	2 Officers sent to open dressing station at BRANDHOEK with equipment & personnel of a tent division for receiving sick & wounded. Qrs to MR-T	
8.30 P.M. May 4th	Lieut. Jas Rogers-Tillstone was sent to casualty clearing station (sick) having injured a toe(?) Onward. List of Officers. Major Good. Major T.H. Payfair. Lieut J.M. Johnston. Lieut Geo. Greene. Lieut 10.73 Keith Lieut J.S. Ward Lieut C.H. Gregory Lieut H.G. Rice Lieut (Q Master) H.C. O'Neill } Temporary Comm. } Transferred from	Transferred from

WAR DIARY or INTELLIGENCE SUMMARY

Army Form C. 2118.
81st Field Ambulance, 27th Division, Expeditionary Force.

Hour, Date, Place	Summary of Events and Information	Remarks and references to Appendices

	Officers	R.A.M.C. M.O.	QMS	S.Sgt	Sgts	Corpls	Privates	A.Cafts	Ashfalters	A.S.C. Sgt	A.S.C. Farriers	A.S.C. Drivers	A.S.C. M.T. Sgt	A.S.C. M.T. Other Ranks	Horse Riding	Horse H.D.	Motor Cycle	Motor Ambulances	Wagon Ambulances	G.S. Wagons	Forage Carts	Water Carts "Maltese"	Wagons General
POPERINGHE – Continued – May 4·15	10	1	1	2	10	9	144	1		3	2	35	1	12	14	45	1	7	3	6	1	3	4

Lt. Grierson returned from H.Q. 27th Div. at POTIJZE 2 P.M. J/E being attached there for 10 days. He did excellent ambulance work.

The Bearers went to collect wounded from the 27th F. Div. Front at 7 P.M. Lieuts Rice & Gregory returned after relieving two R.M.O's at the Ypres front for two days.

7.30 P.M. May 5·15 — Recommended 336 Sgt. H.W. Brown, & 2304 Pte A.E. Wright for Cross order of St George (Russian) 4th Class — to gallants at YPRES on 20th April 1915.

2 A.M. Lieut J.S. WARD of this unit during the night att was wounded by Shrapnel Broken Index finger left hand. Sent to Hospital. (Casualty clearing).

9.30 A.M. In accordance with instructions, Major Peyton proceeded to POPERINGHE to open dressing station with full Tent division personnel & equipment of No 1 section at the Rue de BOESCHEPE Convent presently occupied by No 3 Clearing hospital. About a dozen stalls daily are shown.

WAR DIARY or **INTELLIGENCE SUMMARY.**

81st Field Ambulance, 27th Division, Expeditionary Force.

Army Form C. 2118.

Hour, Date, Place	Summary of Events and Information	Remarks and references to Appendices
continuing May 5. 15	Into POPERINGHE but not in the area of shrapnel shells.	
at R.A.P.	The Officers left bearer parties are shelled out; Lt Green was sent immediately to retain fresh road wounded.	Very necessary as there were many casualties. JW
	At 7 pm request for motor lorry Lt Green & Lt Browne & field 1000 yds south of Ypres party were ordered to stand by, in case of necessity. As.	
May 6. 15	Sent 6 Rooms at POPERINGHE 5.30 PM, & remained until 2.30 AM	
May 7. 15	At 1.30 AM message from A.D.M.S. for Lt Green to bring in bearer party. Motor complete with stretcher bearers were sent for conveyance of bearers since this hut a distance of 7½ miles to walk. Over 200 wounded + 70 sick admitted.	JW
	An officer with 6 men are in the Cellar at the Sick Bastion on MENIN Rd. This place acting as a collecting Station for sick + wounded in the immediate front. and the wounded + sick also drained of many, & await night ambulance for evacuation to dressing station.	
	I went to the dressing station at Poperinghe 10 pm, the place is being heavily shelled but not an immediate area. Being many wounded 4 miles from each, few beerer at 2 AM to 5 AM to 5 o'clock. Dogs a visit as is arranging evacuate convoys. Shells still going one, one shatty the roof, so decided to evacuate at once to Farm G.15.d.9.9. 1000 yds South of Poperinghe. The place was prepared for eventualities. Every wounded & sick & one spent	

(9 29 6) W 4141-468 100,000 9/14 HWV Forms/C. 2118/10

WAR DIARY
or
INTELLIGENCE SUMMARY

81st Field Ambulance, 27th Division, Expeditionary Force.

Army Form C. 2118.

Instructions regarding War Diaries and Intelligence Summaries are contained in F. S. Regs., Part II. and the Staff Manual respectively. Title pages will be prepared in manuscript.

(Erase heading not required.)

Hour, Date, Place	Summary of Events and Information	Remarks and references to Appendices
May 7. 15	wounded on hand, we like 37 halt us to the farm. I at once helped A to M.E. That all we clear without a casualty	
May 8.15	At 2 am bearers wounded through the Shrouds (a Maxim gun) not an hand, It is evacuated. BRANDHOEK which hitherto was as a small ampu going SE E is acting as the main dressing stat: both Two Tents Sub divs working attended 24 from. The interior of the beaver are at Farm 615C79 The Farm acting as a main station for transl—utilities in Farm close by. Brandhoek School is very similar from the Farm dressing Room which is divided up into 5 compartments where wounded can be dressed. 1 at one time. Nursing Orderlies Drivers Stretcher bearers, Officers, nurses over. Accommodate for 60 shezzo sits can close by room for 6 sheltd & 6 sitters. this is used for Officers. Kurs beds 3 blankets when we left open all night. In sultry cases, 8 a framing for 3 min accommodate is used. 250 Sitters.	
May 5.15	The clearing station & wounded from R aid Post. After the heavy fighting all emins to Brandhoek, where by the precticely all eminis to the convoy we are able to keep it by collect evacuation by The Convoy we are able to keep it clear even having more than 200 in at one time. The 1st convoy arrive 11 pm 2nd 2 am 3rd 6 am at 4th 9 am. The Bristol Red Cross Convoy evacuate. We praise the mighty. They always bring as many cars as wanted	

WAR DIARY
81ST FIELD AMBULANCE, 27TH DIVISION, EXPEDITIONARY FORCE
INTELLIGENCE SUMMARY
(Erase heading not required.)

Hour, Date, Place	Summary of Events and Information	Remarks and references to Appendices
May 2, 15	Are required to as often as called for. D.A.D.M.S. 5th Corps supervising this work. This is the most important point in removal of sick & wounded. Convoy must be continuously overrun after the patient has been previously seen. Antiseptics, hot drink & food if advisable, wet clothes removed, get him warm & well blanketed. **Blankets.** When casualties are big & the weather cold an enormous unlimited supply of blankets are essential. We found the 200 or so in 9 store cupboard equipped very useful. I found 2 per patient often necessary whilst up to this which were allowed by the Convoy. The Motor Ambulances are given as 5 per car, in addition for 16 or two. This in extra way, that. The Field Ambulance supply & blanketed stretchers is depleted. The returning convoy this is depleted of blankets & stretchers, given a shortic in return to the are used by the patients. So first 2 reason to send to Casualty Clearing to be first day after the patients have been sent down to them. This appears to be the only quick method of replenishment.	[signature] [signature]

WAR DIARY
or
INTELLIGENCE SUMMARY.

81st FIELD AMBULANCE,
27th DIVISION,
EXPEDITIONARY FORCE.

Army Form C. 2118.

(Erase heading not required.)

Hour, Date, Place	Summary of Events and Information	Remarks and references to Appendices
May 10.15	I learn Pte Ruthen was wounded through the elbow which collects wound & he has been evacuated.	
May 11.15	From G 11 A 3.3 "shot" made for Brandhoek & taken on with a view to acting as an overflow in case of necessity. The site of the mounted Area an Ban Pere Huts. Mot personal out LECOLE BIEN F.Amdt with spare men mostly to patients. The kennels and 14 t no officers about 250 steet are a tonite are allowed to here during the day.	
May 12.15	Many visits for Com hr's most of which were unhelpful so Sect-C the 73rd F.M. Amale (Ree SI) Red (state) so to not to exonerate: Pressing for RMO's here no daily routh, a Corn Sect full to each RMO, the his forward a much satisfactory way of keeping the supplies during present fighting. This Ambulance is supply the whole Division Mos, to Aung weat as an Advanced dept of Medical Stores, to attempt to render us immobile, I am I Opinion that these should be a do out Motor clorry attacked to this Division to the expire use of state canying front	

WAR DIARY or INTELLIGENCE SUMMARY.

Army Form C. 2118.

81st FIELD AMBULANCE,
27TH DIVISION,
EXPEDITIONARY FORCE.

(Erase heading not required.)

Hour, Date, Place	Summary of Events and Information	Remarks and references to Appendices
May 12·15	We added men equipment & bivouac. Sent a letter to Major General Friedrich Bul Socka (Wien and most useful to point who knows Enoch well & met etc) Station. The lorry cars also to used to collect Silly cases & convey bearers. Property. The bearers have to be carried & & from the dressing State in artillery wagons; the ordinary being often 7 miles to the rear, part for the dressing State.	Ford
May 13·15	The storm continued the collects of wounded it become 1/12/24. 1st, 81st, 71st & 73rd. Showed up & it being 3rd night, but 1/2/25 of. Major State. Still to be seen by the 81st. This is quite say. Since the Motor Ambulance have all parked & Started for our place the 73rd Field Ambulance, & ended at the collecting Ambulance and repaid at dusk to put up the bearers.	Ford
May 14·15	Gas Cases. Relief was tried but has not been much use. I have in my possession Hyp Tab Atropin + Morph. Too op they appeared to return in Some cases — & though the Amphinitris dose not the Myor Cough, Sgt Am to internally was useful. Hypo for out. get seem objectionable.	Ford
May 15·15	Bronchitis much better only one Expect bag in state District.	Ford
May 19·15	G O C & started the Brigade at 2 the trenches, but did not visit the medical units.	Ford

HWV Forms/C. 2118/10

WAR DIARY or INTELLIGENCE SUMMARY

81st Field Ambulance, 27th Division, Expeditionary Force.

Army Form C. 2118.

Hour, Date, Place	Summary of Events and Information	Remarks and references to Appendices
May 19.15.	Germans bid eales for "Gallants" in the recent fights quoad & Staff Kirk. Mentioned for ability over also 5 others rank & mentioned + SCM.	front
May 22.15.	Not a heavy round Yrenville, but the horses has been in hard rain & the mud & a camp 1½-2 miles in places. Vk Wright Stretch bearer permit ½ minimum value as guide & as ample to cheer the Otter bearer along.	front
May 24.15	Wire received from A Down "An actin on a large scale has developed East of Ypres — all units should be prepared to concentrate; tents is to say be ready to perform ordinary removes, but 24 hours need be improved. Inv8. all available wagons were packed up ept. the one tent Sub at Porrend Hoek, so that we could move within 2 hours.	front
May 25.15	In b late zone	
May 26.15	The DDt. trupid. an order to the trenches, & they are to be retired tonight, only a small bearer party sent out	front

Army Form C. 2118.

WAR DIARY
or
INTELLIGENCE SUMMARY.

81st FIELD AMBULANCE,
27th DIVISION,
EXPEDITIONARY FORCE.

Part II.

(Erase heading not required.)

Hour, Date, Place	Summary of Events and Information	Remarks and references to Appendices
May 27.15	Orders for Ambulance that we are to move on once. This Ambulance to follow up the 11th Bde (Infantry). The Bde from BRANDHOEK is called BRANDHOEK in is to join the HQ of Ambulance at Farm G.15.C.7.9.	
May 28.15	Whole Ambulance proceeded to LOCRE Slab - J Ann. Bivouaced for the night.	
May 29.15	Proceeded to a Farm South of STEENWERCK to Bivouac here for night.	
May 30.15 to June 1.15	Took a motor Ambulance but enemy dine & made arrangements with O.C. 16th Field Ambulance to take us over from them at 12 noon Today. Two Officers 2 NCOs & 2 men stayed the night at the Advanced Dressing Station CHAPELLE D'ARMENTIÈRES. to learn the work. Major Pen Keyston die. We arrived ERQUINGHEM Posts. HMgr Pen Keyston die. We arrived ERQUINGHEM 9 A.M. dining B. Section to take over from "B" Sect 16th Field Amblce. The Rest Sta. & Bath at BAC St MAUR. Informed HQ 11th Brigade & on arrival. Sick & wounded at the Factory prepared to receive ERQUINGHEM	

WAR DIARY

**81st Field Ambulance,
27th Division,
Expeditionary Force.**

INTELLIGENCE SUMMARY

(Erase heading not required.)

Army Form C. 2118.

Hour, Date, Place	Summary of Events and Information	Remarks and references to Appendices
May 31.15.	Officers admitted — 124 Admitted NCOs & men — 3707 To C. & C.S.T. — 103 „ Fd. Amb. — 15 „ Duty — 2 „ Died — 3 „ Remain — 1 Total — 124 To C. & C.S. — 2575 „ Field Amb. — 975 „ Duty — 107 „ Died — 30 „ Remain — 23 Total — 3707 Officers — 124 Wounded — sick 89 Gas poisoned — 32 — 3 Total — 124 NCOs & men — 3707 Wounded sick — 2411 Gas asp. — 1081 — 215 Total — 3707 To Field Ambulances — 81st Field Ambulance who were sent to Rest Station, an enormous amount of wastage has been noted to this Division, the main cases being sent their owing to C.& C. State. The slow running down not noticeable the many who were retained.	

121/7053

27/4/15 Kaveen

81st Field Ambulance
Part VI
June 15.

June 15

WAR DIARY or INTELLIGENCE SUMMARY

81st Field Ambulance, 27th Division, Expeditionary Force.

Army Form C. 2118.

Instructions regarding War Diaries and Intelligence Summaries are contained in F.S. Regs., Part II. and the Staff Manual respectively. Title pages will be prepared in manuscript.

(Erase heading not required.)

Hour, Date, Place	Summary of Events and Information	Remarks and references to Appendices
June 1. 15.	A Field Ambulance is now attached to the Inf. Bde. Brigade. The men of course is to replenish losses. Transport cleared up the transport & matters of opinion. Since transport & the men is much greater than the one Inf. Regt. This section in expected & accumulates 200 by & cases & 300 sick etc. + motr. collars in the mountains. Replacement one hour reserved + practice meals in mvz.	
June 2. 15.	On recent of the Field Amble a short note. A Training Programme is called up by [?] to include the following details 2 drill parades 5 route march 3 per week & Lectures & Recreation with when received from D.G.58th Officers especially the newly joined officers. 3 lectures a week upon schooling chemical to have General Elliss & General Admirable. work. Equipment & stores wanted on the Temporary command. Thus I find my army training when the time not but my army training officers are sent schools is a Field Ambulance whatsoever, an ex R.M.O.	

Army Form C. 2118.

WAR DIARY
81ST FIELD AMBULANCE, 27TH DIVISION, EXPEDITIONARY FORCE.
INTELLIGENCE SUMMARY.
(Erase heading not required.)

Instructions regarding War Diaries and Intelligence Summaries are contained in F.S. Regs., Part II. and the Staff Manual respectively. Title pages will be prepared in manuscript.

Hour, Date, Place	Summary of Events and Information	Remarks and references to Appendices
June 2.15	The bearer division parties remained but more supervised out trees transferred to a field ambulance.	[initials]
June 3.15	Set a time of aid posts & advanced dressing station near sprinkles for a trench sanitate point of view to be seen some by divisions.	[initials]
June 4.15	Meet SAPNS, + the enemy above points; pleis, + statement. Both being the chief depends. General discussion, against fever, wounds & dysentery. Meat half rate the fly gaurd. Pacific & Chinese flies was suggested for the posts Smile Mosquitoes were prevalent. (Summary Malaria being found since we had so much recurrent Malaria in the division in units of the troops come for India. Mulls + China). Sice & treated of the seriously ill. The following precept to be made here are of Acid Pauretic 50 pts. Sqm. Soaps 3 lbs. Watic to /pts.	[initials]

WAR DIARY or INTELLIGENCE SUMMARY

Army Form C. 2118.

81st Field Ambulance, 27th Division, Expeditionary Force.

Hour, Date, Place	Summary of Events and Information	Remarks and references to Appendices
June 8.15	As Report. Admoni & Bishop took Kapt for Ghain.	
June 9.15	Paint indents for F.S. tremeur, & ft Transport Wagon, also a wood for the making of Tilt tremeur, as these will be of immense use in carrying an bulky equipt. the G.S. wagon do not hold the Shelues load safely. Tilt trams will also preserve the Tilts & lead to reduction & utility.	
June 10.15	2 Officers & 5 NCOs to 37th Field Amblce arrival for materials. Lt Greene, the unit appointed Representative from the 81st Brigade. Requests apparels & officering Amdet. to Antony Reynolds, Lt Potter (TC) & Lieut Belgrade (T.F.) – Deniere, the unit Posted to the unit.	
June 12.15	NCOs from [?] are to be given leave in small batches of about 5 per week. This is much appreciated, as the men have worked well under very trying circumstances.	

Form/C. 2118/10

WAR DIARY
or
INTELLIGENCE SUMMARY.
(Erase heading not required.)

81ST FIELD AMBULANCE,
27TH DIVISION,
EXPEDITIONARY FORCE.

Army Form C. 2118.

Hour, Date, Place	Summary of Events and Information	Remarks and references to Appendices
Jan 13. 15	Col Porran Adms inspected the HQ of the Ambulance at STEENWERCK; also the post Station at BAC ST MAUR and was complimentary.	Good
Jan 14. 15	Lt Edgardo is posted to the 28th Amm Park METEREN with a moving vehicle. Where drivers etc & equip'ts supplied (only Temp'y attached duty) from the Ambulance.	Good
Jan 15. 15	Submitted a list of items I all species at all Species in our Red Cross Stores to any General Quartpork. The person Has accumulate to 200 minor articles with have authority to reding in 150. There are about 100 in at present. Games, libraries, Chocolate, Sweets, Fruit & many Non Ration + Non Ordinary Supplies have been given to m.h. by the British Red Cross Society, Comforts, & Games forms the major part of the Trenchart Items. It has been deemed necessary to cease the batter here, as ERQUINGHEM Road much better accessible to is more central.	Good

Forms/C. 2118/10

Army Form C. 2118.

WAR DIARY
81st FIELD AMBULANCE,
27TH DIVISION,
or
INTELLIGENCE SUMMARY. EXPEDITIONARY FORCE.

(Erase heading not required.)

Instructions regarding War Diaries and Intelligence Summaries are contained in F.S. Regs., Part II. and the Staff Manual respectively. Title pages will be prepared in manuscript.

Hour, Date, Place	Summary of Events and Information	Remarks and references to Appendices
June 15.15	Cooking at the Rest Station is the difficulty. An variety of foods for an attached men made exact judgt. Roasts. Puddings. An improved oven is being run well. Menu. Major Peyton who is in charge is being especially good work by his Keenness & ingenuity. The troops by T.M.s the patients are kept in serum averaging abt 5 days, but its inmates could be sent to reform unit if urgency arose. The Moto Ambulance except for the front line work are absolute at rest, as many as the workshop can take is now being overhauled & painted. The hosed Ambulance wagons are being (nhst also) found that G.S. wagons with the tilts over, do excellently for convey in inter cases to the Rest Station, in the way saving rubber tyres & technical vehicles.	good good
June 21.15	Lieut-Helliton (TC) has been sent to 1st Lewts to R.M.O. Lieut Durban TC replaces. Lennie. good	good

Form/C. 2118/10

Army Form C. 2118.

WAR DIARY
81st FIELD AMBULANCE,
27TH DIVISION,
EXPEDITIONARY FORCE.
or
INTELLIGENCE SUMMARY.
(Erase heading not required.)

Instructions regarding War Diaries and Intelligence Summaries are contained in F. S. Regs., Part II. and the Staff Manual respectively. Title pages will be prepared in manuscript.

Hour, Date, Place	Summary of Events and Information	Remarks and references to Appendices
Jan 22.15	500 ounces Helmark placed text in a reserve.	
Jan 23.15	An A.S.C. opinion from G.H.Q. requested the M.O. of one Ambulance, this is the first opportunity given here (only in the Methodology of prisons) I think it would be better if a Monthly Routine Inspection was carried out. There were many points which required attention. The Car will benefit greatly by this suggestion, & open criticism.	
Jan 27.15	Road (Talc) Curse Car now be taken to should ought to be fit for duty within 10 days, then I think the Ford State 2 much more suitable for much writing work Cars to be always stated. Scabies on the increase as when they arrive they have many times a 5-minute soapy accompany. and the 3 days of Gandeveen Sub Perm treatment Potass Sulphurate Baths the only been of curative value. good	

Form C. 2118/10

31ST FIELD AMBULANCE,
27TH DIVISION,
EXPEDITIONARY FORCE.

Army Form C. 2118.

WAR DIARY
or
INTELLIGENCE SUMMARY.
(Erase heading not required.)

Instructions regarding War Diaries and Intelligence Summaries are contained in F.S. Regs., Part II. and the Staff Manual respectively. Title pages will be prepared in manuscript.

Hour, Date, Place	Summary of Events and Information	Remarks and references to Appendices
June 30. 15	A blood film is being taken from all cases suspected or suffering from Malaria, and a weekly return being made to D.M.S. Also No Stoppencia [?] of all Venereal cases contracted locally. [signed] Summary. This has been a month of delegate work by all Ranks. Peace time training has been its object & aim. Sick convalescent have been very low. The whole personnel, horses, transport, vehicles & equipment are now all made good & serviceable. At first it appeared welcome to Catmenn [?], but the men now appear to quite as much a well the Authorities. [signed]	

Army Form C. 2118.

21ST FIELD AMBULANCE,
27TH DIVISION,
EXPEDITIONARY FORCE.

WAR DIARY
or
INTELLIGENCE SUMMARY.
(Erase heading not required.)

Instructions regarding War Diaries and Intelligence Summaries are contained in F.S. Regs., Part II. and the Staff Manual respectively. Title pages will be prepared in manuscript.

Hour, Date, Place	Summary of Events and Information	Remarks and references to Appendices

	Remaining		Admitted		To C C S		To D R S		Died		To Duty		Remaining	
	Officer	OR	Officer	OR	Officer	OR	Officer	OR	Officer	OR	Officer	OR	Officer	OR
Sick	1	22	12	362	11	182	2	184	-	-	-	7	-	11
Wounded	-	1	3	68	3	52	-	7	-	4	-	3	-	1
"	1	23	15	430	14	234	2	194	-	4	-	10	-	11

The above is a monthly state for the Divisional Station.

	Remaining		From Main Field Ambulance Admitted		To C.C.S.		To Main Field Ambulance To D.R.S		Died		To Duty		Remaining	
	Officer	OR	O	OR	O	OR	O	OR	O	OR	O	OR	O	OR
Sick	-	-	-	645	-	139	1	6	-	1	-	369	-	130
Wounded	-	-	-	26	-	6	-	-	-	-	-	10	-	10
Total	-	-	-	671	-	145	1	6	-	1	-	379	-	140

The above is monthly state for the Main Rest Station.

Many of the evacuations to CCS were Scabies & Eye Cases apart from being seen by the ADMS.

121/7055

27th Division

July '15

34th Field Ambulance

Vol VII

July 15.

Army Form C. 2118.

WAR DIARY
81ST FIELD AMBULANCE, 27TH DIVISION, EXPEDITIONARY FORCE.
or
INTELLIGENCE SUMMARY.
(Erase heading not required.)

Instructions regarding War Diaries and Intelligence Summaries are contained in F. S. Regs., Part II. and the Staff Manual respectively. Title pages will be prepared in manuscript.

Hour, Date, Place	Summary of Events and Information	Remarks and references to Appendices
July 3.15	A report sent to A.D.M.S. Colles recommended Emery units in it near the Brasserie Stables & Advanced Dressing Station.	good
July 6.15	An order 67. R.A.M.C. went by A.D.M.S. 5000 rounds of ammunition to be kept in stock at Bn Rest Station in case of emergency to train to Combatants in Bn Rest Station.	good
July 7.15	Lieut Buchan is posted to 9th Royal Scots.	good
July 10.15	Wheeled Stretchers 3 were moved to the Ambulance about Apr 10th & others in Ypres, they have proved of immense value in expediting the removal of wounded to our Ambulance.	good
July 12.15	Mental Cases A.D.M.S. & other 75. 2 Mental Cases arrive at Nellie Pooh 11 am & just 10 of Mental Cases. 75 % of Mental Cases sent to the Expeditionary Force in accompanied by any Statement of their Case.	good

Forms/C. 2118/10

(9 29 6) W 4141—463 100,000 9/14 H W V

WAR DIARY
or
INTELLIGENCE SUMMARY. FIELD AMBULANCE,
27TH DIVISION,
EXPEDITIONARY FORCE.

(Erase heading not required.)

Army Form C. 2118.

Instructions regarding War Diaries and Intelligence Summaries are contained in F.S. Regs., Part II. and the Staff Manual respectively. Title pages will be prepared in manuscript.

Hour, Date, Place	Summary of Events and Information	Remarks and references to Appendices
July 12·15	and full particulars are called for of all such cases. Lieut Keith (a medic specialist in civil life) of the unit drew up the attached pro forma, & the RMO's were supplied with same.	*Appd*
July 14·15	Number kept in the Field Ambulance. An order that Field Ambulances are not to have more than 20 cases remaining in hospital pending No 82 RAmb [?] RO & DMS. The Red State to be used to its fullest capacity. After our month opening I think this very sound.	*Appd*
July 16·15	Dr Lister "A" & "B" sects moved from ER QUING HEM to St Rest State BAC ST MAUR to take over the Schools at STEEN WERCK from the 37th Field Ambulance, & prepare it for the 81st Bde Staff. Dr Red State owing to the 81st Brigade being in the trenches "C" sect opened a dressing state at the School of Marie East end of ER QUIN HEM, which the 19th Field Ambulance were quitting in accord with Brigade moves. The faction remains held by no less than one by the Brig [?] The "A" Sects Dr Brown's Billets is well appointed, &	

WAR DIARY or INTELLIGENCE SUMMARY

31ST FIELD AMBULANCE,
27TH DIVISION,
EXPEDITIONARY FORCE.

Army Form C. 2118.

Hour, Date, Place	Summary of Events and Information	Remarks and references to Appendices
July 16.15	Capable of accommodating 200 lying in and 300 sitting by return ambulance and bother arrival. The Maire has given his help and emergency aid. There is an excellent cellar Church & will billet 30 Stretcher cases. There is also an advanced Dressing Station at CHAPELLE D'ARMENTIERES as before. This has also a personal of one Officer and NCO & 6 men, & equipment, with one large Mtc Ambulance stands to. Collection is done by day in Service cars, but a night evacuation about 5pm is carried out continuously from the Aid Posts. H.Q. of Mtc Ambulance lives at STEEN WERCK. 4 motor army tran. The Advanced Dr. Posts being a great factor. There are it is thought, adequate for 2 rests of First Ambulance & no much transport, as present to be in the West side of the River LYS as there are only two bridges spanning the River, 3½ miles apart. Then again the Post Station is out of the combat zone & First Guns & so the Positions. As getting the pure tranquil of a chance of all things, the STEEN WERCK School regime is full of cheerers, the White wash, scrubbing brushes, being the chief items & request arb at the Sanit Unit 6 White wards brushes to a whole Field ambulance and orderlies. S ... maty ...	

WAR DIARY or INTELLIGENCE SUMMARY.

(Erase heading not required.)

Army Form C. 2118.

81ST FIELD AMBULANCE,
27TH DIVISION,
EXPEDITIONARY FORCE.

Hour, Date, Place	Summary of Events and Information	Remarks and references to Appendices
July 17. 15	Work not very quickly & am in excellent use. Accommodation is made for 200 patients. Together with a compound to take 20 Serbian cases. (16 cases & Serbian appear to be always with us in an Hospital). The strain on staff is but the hot weather & work is most trying. Admission of sick is now few. 100 cases weekly on average. A Charcoal iron has been bought and of importance for the ironing of Serbian & Lice infected clothes. It has proved of great use. We now form part of the 1st & 15th Armies. Latrines. There are 4 Good Sound Forces (empties) three on pull & smells. Arrangements for Latrines, cysts, of emptying, obtaining (morning will be instituted as far available found; all provided by 44 Salvage. The persons sanitation of the place has been neglected. Milk & Eggs Authority is given to purchase same for the use of patients, No personal or supply officers are ——— has weekly accounts.	
July 21. 15	The Sanitary Sects on Fort at work opening up the main but check a brook it is a huge broken drain 4 ft high but choked & block with mud & stinking clothes, must	

Forms/C. 2118/10

WAR DIARY 21ST FIELD AMBULANCE,
or 27TH DIVISION,
INTELLIGENCE SUMMARY. EXPEDITIONARY FORCE.

Army Form C. 2118.

(Erase heading not required.)

Hour, Date, Place	Summary of Events and Information	Remarks and references to Appendices
July 21. 15	The Engineers have now opened up the Outlet ditch leading to the river. This work is big task, but will be of immense Hygienic value when complete. The fouled ground of the old latrines is in such close proximity to the huts, that so out of good lime has been proved over the whole area executed by it.	
July 28. 15	Cases have been arriving at Premuren train at the Rly Station. Arrangements are being made to obtain field Ambulances to meet them so as to arrive there at 2. P.M. The average admissions per day are 3 etc.; & these come about 12 men to Cooks and Indians etc. etc. These are in poor health, have been arranged in the Plains & its rate is that money are being protest must have a bath & an extension of clean clothing given. To erect clothes as arriving for this etc. a small French Box has been loaned; this is an absolute necessity. The Rly Station Station Sentries Frenchie cannot be approved. Cannot act.	

Jones

81st FIELD AMBULANCE,
27TH DIVISION,
EXPEDITIONARY FORCE.

Army Form C. 2118.

WAR DIARY
or
INTELLIGENCE SUMMARY.
(Erase heading not required.)

Hour, Date, Place	Summary of Events and Information	Remarks and references to Appendices
July 29.15	The Rest Station Sunday arrangements are now perfected, and work satisfactory. A Day Room & Dining Room combined has been installed - a well lighted room, & the floor being used for the purpose. The C R E has been most anxious to help us, & has given timber for Athletic Benches, Trestle Tables, Stand for Potential Camp Kettle which act as dressers in peglises. Tubs for bath. Gratings for same, Shelves etc. Fortunately we have several Cabinet-makers & carpenters in the unit. A piano has been hired, but authority cannot be granted for payment out of imprest, so that in this is good. Two good concerts weekly are given as there is good talent room at hand. Dances are patronised by many officers notables. The S.S. General.	Mard ____ Kmd
July 30.15	Officers Rest St/Stn: a house situated undeniable by the owner, expects & accomodating 11 sick officers bed down at rest. It is a delightful place & meets the need splendidly.	

(9 29 6) W 4141—463 100,000 9/14 H W V Forms/C. 2118/10

Army Form C. 2118.

81ST FIELD AMBULANCE,
27TH DIVISION,
EXPEDITIONARY FORCE.

WAR DIARY
or
INTELLIGENCE SUMMARY.
(Erase heading not required.)

Instructions regarding War Diaries and Intelligence Summaries are contained in F.S. Regs., Part II. and the Staff Manual respectively. Title pages will be prepared in manuscript.

| Hour, Date, Place | Summary of Events and Information | Remarks and references to Appendices |

	Remaining		Admitted		To CCS		To DRS		Died		To Duty		Remaining	
	Officer	O.Rank	O	OR	O	OR	O	OR	O	OR	O	OR	O	OR
Sick	-	11	9	464	4	126	5	311	-	-	-	20	-	18
Wounded	-	-	3	45	3	30	-	*3⁶²ᵗ 5	-	4	-	-	-	3
	-	11	12	509	7	156	5	319	-	4	-	20	-	21

* These were self inflicted wounds sent of a severe nature. Yet.
82ⁿᵈ F.A. look all such cases.
D R S = Div Rest Station.
The above monthly state is for the 81ˢᵗ Field Amb drawing station.

MONTHLY STATE DIV REST STATION

	Remaining		From Oth. Field Amb		To CCS		To Other F.A		Mnt. A Cat		To Duty		Remaining	
	Officer	OR	O	OR	O	OR	O	OR	O	OR	O	OR	O	OR
Sick	-	130	15	834	2	213	-	1	-	111	9	488	-	152
Wounded	4	30	1	22	1	5	-	-	-	12	-	11	4	3
	4	140	16	856	3	218	-	1	-	123	9	499	4	155

Howard

Statement of particulars of:—
No. Rank, Name & Unit

Age
Duration of Mental symptoms
Onset sudden or gradual
Evidence of Hallucinations
    a of hearing
    b of sight
Evidence of Delusion

Has he shown any
    a Suicidal tendencies
    b Homicidal tendencies

Is there any history of fits
    Epileptic
    G.P.I. seizures

Memory
    For recent events
    For remote events

Family history as corroborated by patients:—
    a Insanity or neurotic taint
    b Epilepsy
    c Alcoholism
Exciting cause of Mental attack, e.g.
    Sudden or prolonged mental strain
    Alcoholic excess etc.

M.D. i/c

121/7052

27th Division

8th Field Ambulance
Vol VIII
August 15.

Aug '15

WAR DIARY or INTELLIGENCE SUMMARY

Army Form C. 2118.
81st Field Ambulance, 27th Division, Expeditionary Force.

Hour, Date, Place	Summary of Events and Information	Remarks and references to Appendices
Aug 3. 15.	The 81st Brigade came out of the Trenches last night, & were relieved by the 70th. The 73rd F.A. taking over "C" sect- ions stations at ERQUINGHEM & advanced dressing Stat- ions at CHAPELLE D'ARMENTIERES. "C" Sect. join A. & B. Sects. at H.Q. of the Ambulance. Billets with the rest of the 81st Brigade an rooks in Billets with his rest of the 81st Brigade. Sick daily at 11 & 12 am. some time of the Rest Station. Ambulance go round to the R.M.O's medical magnetic room & collect all sick which are (for Rest Station). A medical Officer always accompany this convoy.	
Aug 4. 15.	Route marches & general training again instituted since their are few to many men in the Ambulance to run the Rest Station, all available given to attend to run the Rest marches. & to go on these Rest marches. This is the dubricate to the personnel to meet adequately the requirements of the Rest Station (Tabulated our but). Run on 7 wards, Large Recruit Room & Drying Room, Sisters Home & Combined Bath House, Pack Store. Quite made Stores Quote Compound, Office, Cook House.	

81ST FIELD AMBULANCE,
27TH DIVISION,
EXPEDITIONARY FORCE.

Army Form C. 2118.

WAR DIARY
or
INTELLIGENCE SUMMARY.
(Erase heading not required.)

Instructions regarding War Diaries and Intelligence Summaries are contained in F.S. Regs., Part II. and the Staff Manual respectively. Title pages will be prepared in manuscript.

Hour, Date, Place	Summary of Events and Information	Remarks and references to Appendices
Aug 4. 15	Officers 3 = 1 Orderly / 1 Medical Clerk / 1 Surgical N.C.O's 8. Nursing Orderlies 14. General duty 14. Batt Horse 3. Washermen 2. Cooks & Corporal 6. Sanitary 6. } This is a medium for place & General Fatigues 24 } rigmen employed fatigues, under N C O 2 } carpenters, whitewashing, etc. Police 9 } There are 3 gals to be kept constantly Office NCO 1 Privates 2. 3 This is exclusive of Transport section Total 90 and 3 Officers	

81ST FIELD AMBULANCE,
27TH DIVISION,
EXPEDITIONARY FORCE.

Army Form C. 2118.

WAR DIARY
or
INTELLIGENCE SUMMARY.
(Erase heading not required.)

Hour, Date, Place	Summary of Events and Information	Remarks and references to Appendices
Aug 5. 15	(ADMS) RO RAMC Aug 4th Strict arrangements have been made that the Sick that Fast Field and Friday, starting from the Strict to evacuate will in future be transferred to Div Rest Station, not any doubtful cases such in field ambulances will be sent in ambulance to be seen by the Strict also Special arrangement for Sgt Cases to be sent to No 4 Station Hopital ARQUES for evacuation, 3 doses a week should there be a Car load. I will comment upon these two points later after I've been seen a difficulties of hypermia, & more to have seen since him. Lieut Hadden (TF) 12 RAMC Probt Lieutenant unit.	good LKE good
Aug 6. 15		
Aug 10. 15	Lieut Hadden posted to RMO 9/Royal Scots. He was forming a Ambulance from in the 9th R.S. & transferred to the RAMC	good
Aug 12.15	Recommended & sent to promote (RAMC) is acc Late Army order. No 1. 7.5th Anglo journaled to ADMS 15 day.	good

WAR DIARY
or
INTELLIGENCE SUMMARY.

81ST FIELD AMBULANCE,
27TH DIVISION,
EXPEDITIONARY FORCE.

Army Form C. 2118.

(Erase heading not required.)

Hour, Date, Place	Summary of Events and Information	Remarks and references to Appendices
Aug 15th	Today have made an inspection of the 81st Brigade Transport lines, and find that ammunition Sanitary precautions are not being observed. Have given the Transport Officer & Serjeant a detailed schema, & remedies. Have been examined & retested water supply & athletes.	
Aug 16th	Again inspected the Transport lines of 81st Brigade & find a marked improvement & all suggestions made have been observed. Attention to the prison in this Article is worthy of comment. Have notified all RMO's in the Brigade that they should when possible make a weekly inspection at least of all their White Area, each in his immediate Area. At 2 o'clock today "B" Mess presented to the "B" Mess of 82nd Field Ambulance Mess in two strong Plates at FORT ROMPU. The F.A. Brigade went into the trenches last night. FORT ROMPU (BRASSERIE) is a very good position & a strong state. Return water. Short.	

WAR DIARY
or
INTELLIGENCE SUMMARY.
(Erase heading not required.)

81st Field Ambulance,
27th Division,
Expeditionary Force.

Army Form C. 2118.

Hour, Date, Place	Summary of Events and Information	Remarks and references to Appendices
Augt 16.15	and ample accommodation for 70 Stretcher & 150 sitters and much more available space if necessary. Most excellent cellars & strong roof. **GRIS POT** There is an advanced dressing station at **GRIS POT** about 1 mile to the the Reg Aid Post. It — meant shelled, but little damage done. A large Dug-out in Eugenia ½ mile nearer its Aid Post, there is a Brewery with excellent cellars at **BOIS GRENIER** The cellars in filthy, but there are great possibilities. Wheeled Stretchers will be of great use there, I shall have sent round leaflets to the troops of MO here is very good. The Aid Posts are in the Communication Trenches, but require improvement. Communication Trenches have been in hand. R.M.O.s have them this in hand.	
Augt 15.15	Visited **FORT ROMPU** Major Pug-Li in command. The place is in good order. Outside arrangements for Latrines, Drench Kitchen are progressing my satisfactorily.	Good

WAR DIARY
or
INTELLIGENCE SUMMARY.
(Erase heading not required.)

Army Form C. 2118.

81ST FIELD AMBULANCE,
27TH DIVISION,
EXPEDITIONARY FORCE.

Hour, Date, Place	Summary of Events and Information	Remarks and references to Appendices
Aug 19.15	Got a line of Aid Posts. Then an H. Batalln in Verb Trench. Sanitati Good, large Dug-outs nearly completed for Aid Posts capable of accomtg 8 stretcher + 12 othr cases. R.M.O.'s Field Thos, Leakis Clynth, Oxygen Glynde with each R.M.O. Movements Shell Shooting, no enemy I find that Aid as Dot-1 2 or 3, no harm reminders or come up to the base at Ypres. Got them all to render a return of the No in hand. Am making them up to 8 Stretcher hrs of Rum to medrs. On Batalln. At advand Dress Stat:— GRIS 'Pot', a big advance in cases, 7 amputies, R.E.'s havng Dug-outs in course of construction with Sand bags of iron Bars. Provided on hulk Sand bags of iron Bars. a fatigue party & being sent tomorw to clean the cellars & whole work the walls of 'B' Salt at BOIS GRENIER, O.C. 'B' Salte his tm in trench. Ngaid.	

WAR DIARY or INTELLIGENCE SUMMARY

81st Field Ambulance, 27th Division, Expeditionary Force.

Army Form C. 2118.

Hour, Date, Place	Summary of Events and Information	Remarks and references to Appendices
Aug 23.14	**Treatment of Burns** R.O. R Anne recd by ADMS No 144 22.8.15 O/C Field Ambulances will arrange & keep supplies Picric Acid (1% Sol) & Carron Oil at advanced dressing stat. & R Aid Posts, & arrange supplies 2 each with the Field Ambulance. I find the best way to treat Burns to RMO's viz: Immediate supplies to be of use is in 2 good Relief Tins one of the men in the unit is a pianist, & he is employed one of them Relief Tins white Red + on one side, and painted Relief Tins white Red + on one side, and painted Carron oil for — on one — & Burns 1% on the other — & Picric Acid 1% for Burns Every Fourteen on his parade me I send for RMO's. Advanced dressing stat. & strong stat = An ample supply of Remedy of Poison Gas is in the possession of each RMO 20 tins each 200 are in the Field Ambulance. — Arnold	

WAR DIARY or INTELLIGENCE SUMMARY

81st Field Ambulance, 27th Division, Expeditionary Force.

Army Form C. 2118.

(Erase heading not required.)

Hour, Date, Place	Summary of Events and Information	Remarks and references to Appendices
Aug 26.15	Asm & Rollo for a Special Trench Stretcher patter one has been submitted today. It is made from a Barraged Behig Stretcher. The bedding is a sufficient for an immense man. a strap could be passed round his chest & fastened to supports. The support does not interfere in the way of the bearer, as would the back of a man sunk in the bearer. Lieut. Cooke TC R Amc posted to the unit.	
Aug 27.15		
Aug 29.15	Inspected Post ROMPu. GRis Pot. + Brewery at BOis GRENIS. the latter has made a much excellent advance being stable, & is Shell Proof against most things except a direct hit by a big shell. It is not occupied by us yet, but is in reserve. & Appts ready should it be necessary. foot.	

Army Form C. 2118.

WAR DIARY 81ST FIELD AMBULANCE,
27TH DIVISION,
or
INTELLIGENCE SUMMARY. EXPEDITIONARY FORCE.

(Erase heading not required.)

Instructions regarding War Diaries and Intelligence Summaries are contained in F.S. Regs., Part II. and the Staff Manual respectively. Title pages will be prepared in manuscript.

Hour, Date, Place												Remarks and references to Appendices

monthly State L. Seaton – GRUITNGHEM

	Remaining		Admitted		To CCS		To DRS		Died		To Duty		Remaining	
	O	OR	O	OR	O	OR	O	OR	O	OR	O	OR	O	OR
Sick	–	16	6	308	1	5	5	314/1835	–	–	–	3	–	–
Wounded	–	3	1	7	–	3	1	7	–	–	–	–	–	–
Total	–	21	7	315	1	11	6	322	–	–	–	3	–	–

monthly State B. Seaton FORT ROMPU

	Remaining		Admitted		from other units		to 82 Hosp		to B.B.St.		to A.R.C.		to G.S.S.		to Duty		to Duty		to 22ⁿᵈ Died of died of Remaining
	officers	o.Rks	officers	o.Rks	officers	o.Rks	officers	o.Rks	officers	o.Rks	officers	o.Rks	officers	o.Rks	officers	o.Rks	officers	o.Rks	officers	o.Rks
Sick	3	147	3	43	20	839	1	27	3	123	10	270	13	608	4	15				
Wounded	1	47	–	1	–	9	1	39	–	4	–	1	–	9	–	3				
Total	4	221	3	44	21	848	1	66	3	124	11	291	13	617	4	159				

monthly State 21st Divisional Rest Station

	Remaining		Admitted		from other units		to 82 Hosp		to B.B.St.		to A.R.C.		to G.S.S.		to Duty		Remaining	
	officers	o.Rks	officers	o.Rks	officers	o.Rks	officers	o.Rks	officers	o.Rks	officers	o.Rks	officers	o.Rks	officers	o.Rks	officers	o.Rks
Sick	4	152	3	43	20	839	–	27	3	123	10	270	13	608	4	156
Wounded	–	3	–	1	1	9	1	39	–	4	1	1	–	9	–	3
Total	4	155	3	44	21	848	1	66	3	124	11	291	13	617	4	159

12/7050

27th Division

81st Field Ambulance

Vol IX

Sept. 15

Sept 15

WAR DIARY
or
INTELLIGENCE SUMMARY.
(Erase heading not required.)

Army Form C. 2118.

81ST FIELD AMBULANCE,
27TH DIVISION,
EXPEDITIONARY FORCE.

Hour, Date, Place	Summary of Events and Information	Remarks and references to Appendices
Sept 1. 15	Yesterday a searching thorough inspection of Horses & Transport vehicles was made by Lt. Col. Liddell, OC ASC Train 27th Divn. Today he furnished a detailed report upon same to us (per ADMS). On the whole the report was good, but pointed out where improvements could be made. This :- **Horses.** Messrs Tait & Cowper require more attention. S Horsey on the whole good, but some are inclined to be a little narrow at the girths. **Harness.** Good Condits. There are 3 sets of limbered wagon G.S. Harness not provided with the necessary harness to attis it to go into an ordinary S.S. wagon. The pole chains are now being procured through properties. 12 rein & D ring of the breast harness, notice of carrier from the centre breast harness. The narrow pieces of harness had been noticed to on HoD but in the meantime be prepared to fit D's at the centre of the breast harness vehicles. all good. Farriers Cart. Too excessive weight. This must be avoided by demanding home shoes at own regular intervals. And shoes in be carried in Forge Cart. All the above points are in hand & will be carried up in detail.	

WAR DIARY
or
INTELLIGENCE SUMMARY.
(Erase heading not required.)

Army Form C. 2118.

81ST FIELD AMBULANCE,
27TH DIVISION,
EXPEDITIONARY FORCE.

Hour, Date, Place	Summary of Events and Information	Remarks and references to Appendices
Sept 1. 15	Advanced Dressing Station. Voila ARIS POT and just everything in good order also all R.A.O.s Aid Posts, delighted has been displayed in the way of whitewashing the Dugouts. Wins, gun's Shelter kept, & a sense of comfort. Drains are being cut around, & provision made for West weather. This A D Slate (Capt Keith) is well versed with Officer i/c Typography, every Officer on him goes up to the A.D.D Slate to ascertain the lie of the land, & medical arrangement. Each Officer makes a map, Aid Posts, 1 - 2 gns of the Trenches, Community Trenches, Aid Posts, Roads. A.D.Slate & Main Dressing Station. It is one of the First Duties of an Officer in charge of A.D. Slate to make his maps of the above points, send to his own use & to the Officer i/c the H Q Field Ambulance Office. And to notify any alteration of Aid Posts, trench Cartridge men notify any alteration of Aid Posts, trench Cartridge. So that it may be added to the maps for reference.	
Sept 3. 15	Capt Greene + Lt & QM O'Kill granted 7 days Leave 3-9-15 to 10-9-15 + 4-9-15 to 11-9-15 respectively. Rifles of Patients. an order, then there are transferred from a Field Ambce to a casualty clearing station, their rifles & Bayonet will be taken from & to a casualty clearing station, their rifles & Bayonet will be taken from & the Armourer Shops 27th DIV.	

WAR DIARY or INTELLIGENCE SUMMARY

Army Form C. 2118.

81st FIELD AMBULANCE,
27TH DIVISION,
EXPEDITIONARY FORCE.

(Erase heading not required.)

Instructions regarding War Diaries and Intelligence Summaries are contained in F.S. Regs., Part II and the Staff Manual respectively. Title pages will be prepared in manuscript.

Hour, Date, Place	Summary of Events and Information	Remarks and references to Appendices
Sept 3. 15	In no case will triflers or persons be sent to a Field Ambulance to a casualty clearing station. Rifles, bayonets & men who are sick to Field Ambulance will be sent direct to Ammunition ship.	
Sept 4. 15	(A.D.M.S. in Lieut) D.A.D.M.S. calls to confer at his office to discuss (in Camera) a scheme for medical arrangements in anticipated & suspected activity on our front. Most meticulous & careful. Informed me that the points discussed were. ADMS at D.W HQ. Dressing Station as at present FORT ROMPR. Advanced Dressing Station. To be moved to GRIS POT & BOIS GRENIER. Bois Grenier (The Brewery) being quite ready & a road sufficient place in the strong cellars will accommodate between 200 & 300 wounded. GRIS POT will be able to keep halt me officer & two men. Dugouts capable of 30 wounded. Communication. R.M.O's keep ADS late informed of numbers etc by Runner & Telephone to Brigade HQ who is in touch the ADS. A Runner belongs to this battalion to be at Brigade HQ. R.M.O's Aid Post will use Battalion Telephone & Brigade HQ.	till available cellars accommodation be prepared.

WAR DIARY
or
INTELLIGENCE SUMMARY.
81st FIELD AMBULANCE,
27th DIVISION,
EXPEDITIONARY FORCE.

(Erase heading not required.)

Army Form C. 2118.

Hour, Date, Place	Summary of Events and Information	Remarks and references to Appendices

Sep 4.15 — Very important message by runner & by wire from R.M.O.s.

Regimental Stretcher Bearers are responsible up to the Aid Posts, Field Ambulance Bearers beyond that point. Should the casualties be very great we give the M.O.'s stretcher bearer help & promise, or if so demand his R.M.O.'s will ask them C.O.'s for more bearers forthwith. The stretcher

Collection of Cases. All cases able to walk will walk to stream side. Bomb will be placed at the corner of the nowadays way to 81st Field Ambulance →. There are roads which ± propos'd now. Rey will be an forming an jumping to in state & preparatic. & in Charge to send N.C.O. forward, or man collected in group, & written details eg:— Proceed with " we will carry injured & stretcher to Stream Side FORT RO MP ar etc. Party, 2, 4 wounded to stream section of A.D.Site.

This will i now much lichen of A.D. Site

The methods to be adopted Except from Aid Pol.

Ambulance Wagon will take the pts for advanced Drenng Stat.

Shortened Stretchers will be used were necessary in the trenches.

Wheeler Stretcher will be in general use 4 to give ease 4 require of constantly.
Front to A.D.Site.

Bearers & Reliefs Pte Major Brents by a Bearer Subaltern will be Kept up by 5 on GRENADIER NCO + NCO s.

3 Tent Sub-divn men. Two Bearer Div'ns Open

WAR DIARY
or
INTELLIGENCE SUMMARY.
81ST FIELD AMBULANCE,
27TH DIVISION,
EXPEDITIONARY FORCE.

(Erase heading not required.)

Army Form C. 2118.

Hour, Date, Place	Summary of Events and Information	Remarks and references to Appendices
Sept 4. 15	A second Bearer Sect. will be in reserve at Straw's Slate FORT ROMPU & it needs be the Third will be ready for this Reat Slate at STEENWERCK to reinforce. Notify A Sun what it has to done. The Reserve Field Ambulance with Adjutants Ambulance Cars to await the wounded in front of attacks by A D.M.S. And will remain central to his Division to stand by in readiness. Normal transport of officers for above. R.M.O.s at Aid Posts. O/C Bearer Sec. & M Officer at Advancing Dressing Slate. Anc Officer at G RIS POT (advanced dressing Slate). Three Officers at Straw's Slate FORT ROMPU (one always on duty.) D/C & QMaster at ---- about Quarters. The Intermediate Point Fort Straw's Slate is intended to send 2/10 Cases from Summatis Billets, Gun Position etc. Clearing all done at Straw's Slate. No attempt at present force to be made at A D Slate; but Patients admits will be passed to all Cellars & all special letter Ant - Tox in; Tournyant, Morphia etc.	BOIS GRENIER

WAR DIARY
or
INTELLIGENCE SUMMARY.

81ST FIELD AMBULANCE,
27TH DIVISION,
EXPEDITIONARY FORCE.

(Erase heading not required.)

Army Form C. 2118.

Hour, Date, Place	Summary of Events and Information	Remarks and references to Appendices
Sept 4. 15	Shirtliffe Bn.Lin will be sent to A.T.S. & I.D.S. RMOs may require more. One Rest Station will send extra Shirtlifs to other units. At Rest Station there are 160 Shirtlifs own & above bolshments equipment for the use of patients. "Most of the Gregory arranged have been typed, & supplies to be from A. & M.S. stores drawn, & informed all Officers & Sgt Majors of this plan."	
Sept 6. 15	Anticipate of activity to commence in day or two. Officers & personnel all probe to see with plans. There are 120 beds in the Rest Station, Am letting slips to send the depends cases of illness down to Corvells Clearing. This will mean about 36, the remainder can march & beyond their limit of a first aid sling, stops a case appears to be unfit for duty, better 2 days, it is the Rest to Corvells Clearing. good.	

WAR DIARY
INTELLIGENCE SUMMARY

Army Form C. 2118.

81ST FIELD AMBULANCE,
27TH DIVISION,
EXPEDITIONARY FORCE.

Hour, Date, Place	Summary of Events and Information	Remarks and references to Appendices
Sept 6, 15	Inspected Rest Posts. Advanced D.S. "B" Section from Slate Fort R.O.M.P.u. all adequate + much to expt with large numbers. GRIS Pot. ten Cake Poznin. 100 poorer Rubi. (Tea, Sugar, Tinned Butter, Bacon etc.) Large ground oto Cubes etc. beside 30 other main Ration. Hot food can be served at once. This is what the personnel approved most. Blanket 50 extra. Plenty strong the ungary Crew only, on the main divining + changing of Rest, but seen if not already done so by R.M.O but to have at FORT R. In Ph. Two large Trusses of Clean Straw in Left of Myself. Three Primus Stoves on the alm too faulty. Wants afternoon inspected every case in Bri Rest Sta. to adjust into accordingly. Ward	
Sept 7, 15	In Slate Dro Amb. Inspl. 50 in Rest Statn. one Blast cspatli + decompensle 120 wounded + prepared + empty. Ready to take in: should recent arrive, although this is not part of the scheme Programme. Ward	

Army Form C. 2118.

WAR DIARY
or
INTELLIGENCE SUMMARY. 81st Field Ambulance,
27th Division,
Expeditionary Force.

(Erase heading not required.)

Hour, Date, Place	Summary of Events and Information	Remarks and references to Appendices
Sept 10.15	Go to see DADMS (ADMS still away on leave) by request to talk over prospects of my being Actg ADMS until ADMS's return on Tuesday 14th. DADMS & being away, to proceed to XIIth Corp Hqr as DADMS. He at the same time asks to proceed to appoint ADMS's return.	
Sept 11th	2 Officers & 21 Other ranks of the 70th Field Ambulance posted to us for instruction. Half of these were sent to FORT ROMPU "B Section" & Advanced Dressing Station. Col MORRIS to see ADMS's 23rd Divn to arrange above matters.	
Sept 12th	S. ADMS leaves to take up duty XIIth Corp. I am Actg ADMS temporarily. Capt Rudkin soon to take up duty as DADMS. All leave is cancelled in the Division. ADMS 23rd Divn came to arrange the next officers & men to be posted to instruction. Orders F/10 23rd Divn are to take over from the 27th Divn the next few days.	

WAR DIARY or INTELLIGENCE SUMMARY

Army Form C. 2118.

81st Field Ambulance, 27th Division, Expeditionary Force.

Hour, Date, Place	Summary of Events and Information	Remarks and references to Appendices
Sept. 13. 15	Army with BA/DMS prepare operation orders for the 23rd Div. Field Ambulance to withdraw and for 27th Div. Field Ambulances to take over from 23rd Field Ambulance: 69th Field Ambulance " " 83rd " 70th " " " 82nd " 71st " " " 81st " with the result that the advanced posts after the 69th Field Ambulance take over from the 81st Field Amb. Advanced posts at FORT ROMPU, GRIS POT & Bois GRENIER respectively, inside the total of the 71st Bryants all going into the Rest Station at the 71st Field Ambulance later on the Rest Station at STEEN WERCK to the 71st. 3 officers including Co. 71st Field Amb. with 81st Field Amb. Ranks attached to no. 81st Field Amb for instruction to take over on the 16th Sept. Avok.	

WAR DIARY
or
INTELLIGENCE SUMMARY.

81ST FIELD AMBULANCE,
27TH DIVISION,
EXPEDITIONARY FORCE.

Army Form C. 2118.

Hour, Date, Place	Summary of Events and Information	Remarks and references to Appendices
Sept 14.	The 69th Field Ambulance (one Section) took over from "B" Section 9th Ambulance FORT ROMPU. GRIS POT Bois Grenier at 2 P.M. taking "B" Section from H.Q. at STEENWERCK. A D M S returned from Bruce this morning.	
Sept 16.	The 71st Field Ambulance Tngr. arr. Rail Stat. STEENWERCK today 2. P.M. Standing over everything as a going concern, only taking own Establishment Equipment — 160 Stretchers have returned to No 2 London Casualty Clearing Station. MERVILLE by order of D M S 3rd Corps. Orders received yesterday for the Ambulance to proceed on the 17th to BETHUNE in Xeno Area (8 miles this side). Now to MERRIS. Have arranged with Brigade (81?) for convoys to follow up troops & pick up stragglers. Have handed over to 71st Field Ambulance 36 Field Cos. of Dick. which here be perfectly well made a week, and to send for them to no dress area of hd.	

WAR DIARY or INTELLIGENCE SUMMARY

Army Form C. 2118.

81st FIELD AMBULANCE,
27th DIVISION,
EXPEDITIONARY FORCE.

Hour, Date, Place	Summary of Events and Information	Remarks and references to Appendices
Sept 16.15	by Car; one of them 36 are cases which only came in today.	
Sept 17.15	A motor Ambulance went round the Billets of the remaining Battalion in the 9th Bgde at 6 A.m to collect any Sick which they wish to send to hospital. The Boer Battalion moved at 7am. 9 Am we proceeded to Farm south of MERRIS & Influta's area; 11 AM. Reported to ADMS at MERRIS. South Officer to get in touch with the Battalion area of our Brigade. 11:15 the ADMS ordered send all M.T. Ambulance, Motor cycle & all Mechanical Personnel to report to D.C. Trains and Workshop Section at 6 pm tomorrow morning. Am Gun ordered to accompany them. Our Motor Ambulance will proceed by Road to New Area, & will carry 3 day Rats. Later Two large Motor Ambulance to remain with us in Charge 1 or 2 staff officers of the unit.	

WAR DIARY
or
INTELLIGENCE SUMMARY   81ST FIELD AMBULANCE,
27TH DIVISION,
EXPEDITIONARY FORCE.

Army Form C. 2118.

Hour, Date, Place	Summary of Events and Information	Remarks and references to Appendices
Sept 18.15	Went to THIENNES (place of entrainment) with DADMS to investigate the Road + the renderings siding for loading. Orders issued for us to entrain THIENNES on the 20th Sept.	
Sept 19.15	Collected such to Bryne Anne (Belts) Seven that to Gazette of Sept 16: to Temp Lt Colonel June 5. 15. Also in Daily Paper of Sept 16th I am promoted Capt Keith to 12th to hit. Awarded the Military Cross.	
4 pm	Orders come stating that we entrain at GUILLANCOURT. AAA	
Sept 21.15	Left THIENNES 14-28 arrived GUILLANCOURT midnight of the 20th. Met by DADMS who motored me to MORCOURT to show me our new quarters, which were prepared by a Field Ambulance what were to move out.	

Army Form C. 2118.

WAR DIARY
or
INTELLIGENCE SUMMARY
(Erase heading not required.)

81ST FIELD AMBULANCE,
27TH DIVISION,
EXPEDITIONARY FORCE.

Instructions regarding War Diaries and Intelligence Summaries are contained in F. S. Regs., Part II. and the Staff Manual respectively. Title pages will be prepared in manuscript.

Hour, Date, Place	Summary of Events and Information	Remarks and references to Appendices
Sept 21.15	4 am Very misty morning. Marched back to GUILLANCOURT & after detraining was completed, we marched to NORCOURT. The FRENCH Ambulance moved out at 6.15 am. This is a large farmhouse used as Farm Buildings. Shortage of Sanitary & Water duties. Rent are possible & great improvement by a few days fatigues. = Accommod: can be made to run a Rest Station for 150 & more by little extension = The day has been given to fatigues and =	
Sept 22.15	The 77th Infantry Brigade are ready in billets at MORCOURT & NARFURZEE-ABANCOURT. 1st Cultr Force being 5 miles away. The Quack Mast E. previous to our arrival insisted this for billets week. ADMS whom I am to be very good for billets & prepare accordly. Rest Station	

Forms/C. 2118/11.

WAR DIARY
or
INTELLIGENCE SUMMARY 31st Field Ambulance, 27th Division,
Expeditionary Force.

(Erase heading not required.)

Army Form C. 2118.

Instructions regarding War Diaries and Intelligence Summaries are contained in F. S. Regs., Part II. and the Staff Manual respectively. Title pages will be prepared in manuscript.

Hour, Date, Place	Summary of Events and Information	Remarks and references to Appendices
Sept 22.15	Inoculate 2 men for tetanus on the grounds of hands & ankles not for Repair. Athletic Benches. Drains. Soak Pits. Kitchen and all available rooms scrubbed with white wash. Removed sand pails to form 100 patients. + 2 motor Sick in Rest Stats. Find well.	
Sept 23.15	An Officer, 6 men & Motor Ambulance write with ett. Regiment open a Record State a WARFUZÉE for the Record 1 Sick & Battalion in that area. They are enough to MORCOURT in the evening. An Officer is handed to test an Moto Ambulance. to F/L Brymts who means. Good.	
Sept 24.15	Mr Rich of the Ambulance to remain packed. Two rooms have been secured close by in wh. to make baths for the troops. Rm is only limited accommodation. Drain & Latrine Supplys for this purpose. Very bad, but intend to make a drain. front	

Army Form C. 2118.

WAR DIARY
or
INTELLIGENCE SUMMARY

81st FIELD AMBULANCE,
27TH DIVISION,
EXPEDITIONARY FORCE.

(Erase heading not required.)

Instructions regarding War Diaries and Intelligence Summaries are contained in F. S. Regs., Part II. and the Staff Manual respectively. Title pages will be prepared in manuscript.

Hour, Date, Place	Summary of Events and Information	Remarks and references to Appendices
Sept 24/15	And filter the water from the river by water carts (3 mile away). Major Reyts has it in hand front.	
Sept 25/15	An Officer proceed to AMIENS to enquire after Château Henderin (Oregon Sten) + Steam succeeded in obtaining same of river. The drain of the Bath House is near complete + will be able to bath 350 a day by evening of the Tubs + C Henderin are gift to Germany.	
Sept 26/15	All the buildings are now in a kentich condition, after strenuous work by the Philipe Nester, & a most excellent Sgt Major (Timmy)ford	
Sept 30/15	In attempt to the 87th Brigade going into the Trenches, I have prepared The MAIRIE as a dressing Station, it is alongside the Rail Siats. It is expected & taking in 30 wounded. The Rooms are mostly strong Rooms making an excellent specially strong Room	

1247 W 3299 200,000 (E) 8/14 J.B.C. & A. Forms/C. 2118/11.

Army Form C. 2118.

WAR DIARY
or
INTELLIGENCE SUMMARY
81ST FIELD AMBULANCE,
27TH DIVISION,
EXPEDITIONARY FORCE.

(Erase heading not required.)

Hour, Date, Place	Summary of Events and Information	Remarks and references to Appendices
Sept 30.15	Busy day. Omi arrives here two Officers have been left it to investigate the Front line. Three Motors for the Field Ambulances in the Front line, 1st Advanced Dressing Station, & same. Tents arrive the afternoon for Baths, arranged per day want to bath 300 Moore. Two Chauffeurs arrive but leaving. Our Field Ambulance personnel took baths this afternoon & evening.	

1247 W 3299 200,000 (E) 8/14 J.B.C. & A. Form/C. 2118/11.

Army Form C. 2118.

WAR DIARY
or
INTELLIGENCE SUMMARY

(Erase heading not required.)

81ST FIELD AMBULANCE,
27TH DIVISION,
EXPEDITIONARY FORCE.

Hour, Date, Place	Summary of Events and Information	Remarks and references to Appendices

Statement from 1st September to 15th September FORT ROMPU.

	Remained		Admitted		To C.C.S.		To D.D. duty		To duty together		Remains	
	offrs	O.Rks	offrs	O.Rks	offrs	O.Rks	offrs	O.Rks	offrs	O.Rks	offrs	O.Rks
Sick	7	169	2	25	2	117		24			2	10
Wounded	3	21	2	20		3		1				
	10	190	4	45	2	120		25			2	10

Monthly Statement September 1915. 21st Divisional Rd. Station

	Remained		Admitted		To other 7 amb.		To C.C.S.		Together		To other 7 a.		To duty		Remains	
	offrs	O.Rks	offrs	O.Rks	offrs	O.Rks	offrs	O.Rks	offrs	O.Rks	offrs	O.Rks	offrs	O.Rks	offrs	O.Rks
Sick	4	156	5	356	8	384	3	312	3	81		3	9	410	2	87
Wounded		3		1		2		1		1				3		1
	4	159	5	357	8	386	3	313	3	88		3	9	413	2	88

Cottage
Dr H Brown
81st F. Ambulance
Oct-15
Vol X

21/7493

WAR DIARY or INTELLIGENCE SUMMARY

Army Form C. 2118.

81st Field Ambulance,
27th Division,
Expeditionary Force.

(Erase heading not required.)

Hour, Date, Place	Summary of Events and Information	Remarks and references to Appendices
Oct 2. 15' MORCOURT	Transit Rest. 6 cases were admitted to Rest S/Cls. How many from 82nd Field Ambulance. 2 an adjusted one ? Two sick cases. A.D.M.S. R.O. 185 calls for a report on all cases as follows:— (1) How long the men have been in the trenches. (2) How often boots & socks have been removed to permit of proper drying & rubbing to feet. (3) How often clean socks had been put on. (4) If boots fit properly. (5) Previous attacks (if any). (6) Previous sick cases (these are the first which have been through our hands since last spring) are as follows:—	

Unit	NO	RANK	Name	Service B.E.F.	How long in Trenches (1)	How oft. boots & socks, etc. (2)	(3)	(4)	(5)
2 DCLI	9915	Pte	Thomas Q	9/12	6 days	once	not at all	Too large	Jan 1915 Trench 2½ days
	(2)			5/12	6 days	removed daily but not pulled	not at all tight	good Tight	nil
	(3)			5/12	6 days				nil
	(4)			4/12	8 days	3 times	3 times	good	nil
	(5)			4/12	7 days	twice	not at all	light	nil
	(6)			10 wks	5 days	once	not at all	tight	nil

Morto

WAR DIARY
or
INTELLIGENCE SUMMARY

81st FIELD AMBULANCE,
27TH DIVISION,
EXPEDITIONARY FORCE.

Army Form C. 2118.

(Erase heading not required.)

Instructions regarding War Diaries and Intelligence Summaries are contained in F. S. Regs., Part II. and the Staff Manual respectively. Title pages will be prepared in manuscript.

Hour, Date, Place	Summary of Events and Information	Remarks and references to Appendices
Nov 2. 15	M and I have issued have the 27th Division Order 697 Oct 1.15 has been observed which reads as follows. With the approach of cold weather all ranks should be warned as to the methods of frostbite preventing (Chilled FEET). A preparate for application 6 feet of Trench Talgo will shortly be available. It is important that particular attention is paid to the proper fitting of boots, which should be loose laced & sufficiently large enough for two pairs of socks to be worn. Boots & socks should be examined as often as circumstances permit, but at least once a day, and the feet warmed by rubbing them. Never sit a fire. Paper wrapped round the feet inside the boots or rubbing of Soda will prevent cold feet. It requires to be changed immediately it gets damp. On leaving the trenches regimental arrangements should be made where possible to provide clean & dry boots, COLD water & soap. It is the purpose of Warming Socks & drying the feet after which dry Socks should be put on. Hot water must on no account be used for this purpose. Pullover sheets should seem be put in supply. I have been to Capt Dr Johnston. If the men met to mentspile we can buy French feet, and further carry out the routine treatment of \"Nash\" in cold water strong Gently with torus. Rub lightly with Methylated Spirit. Apply great medicated Oil 1-40. Swath in wool Large flannel Bed Sock keep patient well warm hot milk-Bovin a fair change hours as often for pain, and Morphine only in very bad cases Good. Reports for Pain, and Morphine only in very bad cases. Good. Milk Cases are to be transported to 83rd Field Ambulance	

Army Form C. 2118.

WAR DIARY
or
INTELLIGENCE SUMMARY
(Erase heading not required.)

81ST FIELD AMBULANCE,
27TH DIVISION.
EXPEDITIONARY FORCE.

Hour, Date, Place	Summary of Events and Information	Remarks and references to Appendices

Oct 2.15 — to the lines busy in treating all defect cases & sending to the Convalescent Camp Slight & will see with this all cases before departure. Maur

Oct 3.15 — Baths. There are thoroughly established.
Equipment: { 150 tubs Chaudières
            { 85 sits Chaudières
            { 12 ½ barrels (Tubs).

Personnel: 1 N.C.O. to work the superior for an
          5 men & 4 fires (part of the lines)

450 men a day are being bathed.

Dental Cases. Received D.M.S. 3rd Army 267/15 — Mart
Care Memo. Provisional Dental Treatment —

Oct 4.15 — The 87th Brigade Ambulance near the Dépôt Section
at 15.27. Div. Front line (today) in consequence two
Officers, 2 N.C.O's & 7 men with the necessary equipment
and one Motor Ambulance (for transport cases) have taken
over the Advanced Dressing Station at CHUIGNES
from the 82nd Field Ambulance who supplied
the medical need to the 82nd Brigade who came out 2

WAR DIARY
or
INTELLIGENCE SUMMARY
(Erase heading not required.)

Army Form C. 2118.

81st FIELD AMBULANCE,
27TH DIVISION.
EXPEDITIONARY FORCE.

Instructions regarding War Diaries and Intelligence Summaries are contained in F. S. Regs., Part II. and the Staff Manual respectively. Title pages will be prepared in manuscript.

Hour, Date, Place	Summary of Events and Information	Remarks and references to Appendices
p.m. 4.15"	The trenches early this morning relieved by the 87th Brigade. "C" Sect: Officers Personnel & equipment Supply, ambulances. The rest of the Advanced Dressing Station. The Main Dressing Station is at H.Q. & H.no. Havent. MORCOURT. The MAIRIE is prepared to receive the wounded, one room ready in excellent opposite the Room. The Mairie & Schools opposite to the Red Slate held by us. Collecting of wounded. The 81st Brigade (so to speak) have a right & left sector. The advanced Dressing Station at CHUIGNES can only clear wounded from the Right Sector owing to communication difficulties, & good roads or weather absence of tracks or roads. The Right Side can be evacuated for the most part by day, then including a long carry to the wagon Rendez vous, but by the use of wheeled stretcher carriers from is very convenient use made easy. To MORCOURT, & not. The Right Sector is cleared direct to CHUIGNES. The Advanced Dressing Station at CHUIGNES. things. The Advanced Dressing Station will be appointed will the front line. All Officers have become well acquainted with the Topography & communication trenches forward	Maps to scale appended.

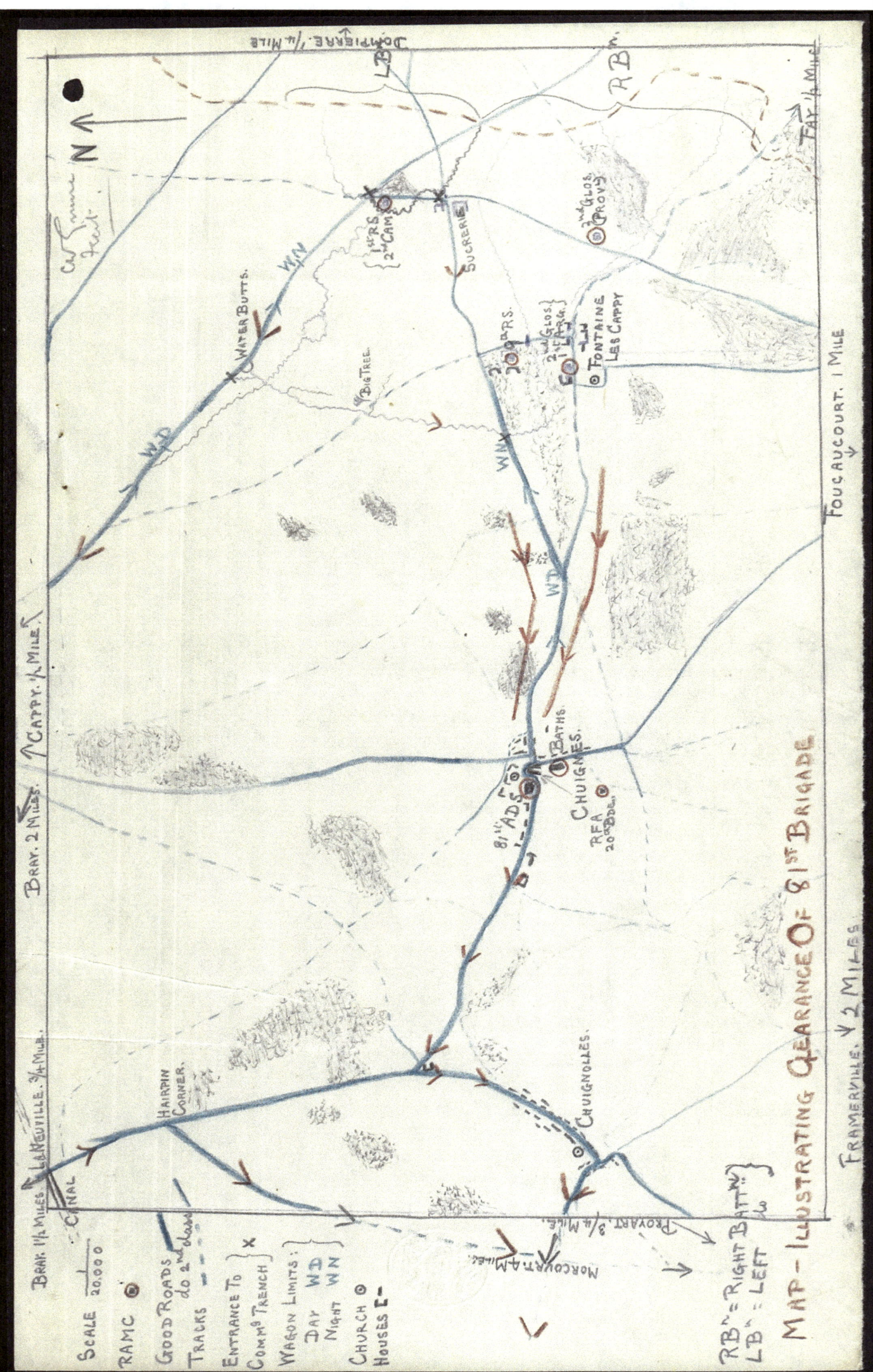

WAR DIARY
or
INTELLIGENCE SUMMARY
(Erase heading not required.)

Army Form C. 2118.

81ST FIELD AMBULANCE,
27TH DIVISION,
EXPEDITIONARY FORCE.

Instructions regarding War Diaries and Intelligence Summaries are contained in F. S. Regs., Part II. and the Staff Manual respectively. Title pages will be prepared in manuscript.

Hour, Date, Place	Summary of Events and Information	Remarks and references to Appendices
1914-15	Waterproof sheets & Corkbars daily. Chauffeurs will all this time have been carried out daily, the last week in anticipation of this Ambulance wearing the Front Line. By experience I find that careful study of maps, especially with regard to Natural Cover, and the becoming thoroughly familiar with the country, roads & power land marks, have saved this unit & many casualties, and successful evacuation of all sick & wounded. The Aid Post on all occasions with all speed possible. Most specially at YPRES (April & May 1915) where Aid Posts changed their positions often daily. The personnel knowledge gained before the great battle commenced still in no invaluable. Every yard of ground covered in the area occupied by this division was traversed on several occasions by the Officer of this unit, Capt. Greene of this unit had such knowledge & acquired this knowledge that he invariably acted as guide, since he possessed marked natural ability in this direction, together with scientific knowledge of map reading.	

WAR DIARY
or
INTELLIGENCE SUMMARY

(Erase heading not required.)

Army Form C. 2118.

81ST FIELD AMBULANCE,
27TH DIVISION,
EXPEDITIONARY FORCE.

Hour, Date, Place	Summary of Events and Information	Remarks and references to Appendices
Oct 5.15. MORCOURT.	Yesterday from the MAIRE & this Village asking for a bottle of the local Remedy to the alleged to the Divn. She doesn't give in a name. The duty won give to me, signed appeared in it R.O. 7/5. O.C. 81 Field Ambulance will be responsible for planning out the Cemetery in accordance with Air Mem. 1575/2 9th Sept. Bayside Chaplain to give every assistance. The planning has been done, carried out. = Last evening 6 P.M. I went forth 2 other officers to collect wounded from the 5th Left Seaforths. I am front. Saw Aid Post of 5th Royal Scots, it is a Dug-out in a Communication trench good to mile down the trench from the Road. Capains G. Hatcher & Reeve Seems surprised with arrangements. 12 rubber cases. (Capt. O'Hanlon M.O./c 1st Royal Scots is an excellent R.M.O. always inspecting his Aid Post & sick surroundings, & awaits the Field Ambulance clearing his cases in every way possible by admitting a stronger understanding with all Bearer Officers. Should I change my Aid Post to notify me at once, & arrange for a guide to conduct Bearer Officer to his new post.) Make Special reference to these points. As R.M.O.s do not always strictly conform to these very important & vital points. The wounded from the 5th Left Seats are brought direct to Dressing Station.	
Oct 6.15. MORCOURT.		

WAR DIARY or INTELLIGENCE SUMMARY

Army Form C. 2118.

81st FIELD AMBULANCE,
27th DIVISION,
EXPEDITIONARY FORCE.

(Erase heading not required.)

Hour, Date, Place	Summary of Events and Information	Remarks and references to Appendices
Oct 6.15 MORCOURT.	After accompanying the Aid Post I proceeded to investigate the Right Sector from the A.D. Stat at CHUIGNES. The Aid Post in this sector is in trees & easy to connect by the aid of wheeled stretcher carriers to the Major Rendezvous.	
Oct 7.15 MORCOURT.	Two officers at the A.D. Stat investigated all the tracks (communications) to see if the left sector could be cleared to CHUIGNES instead of the Corn going the long distance by Road through Cappy, CAPPY. They found it possible, even under cover and by the way, had a 1st Aid Crowle carry. This is being adopted. Since the casualties are light, but showed they at any time became heavier, the Road via CAPPY must be again used, & other Advanced Dressing Statis opened here. Baths are being constructed at the A.D. Stat in trenches about 80 to 100 yards away. A.D.M.S. informed me that evacuation from men marked "B" handed over the personnel of the battln on return. & roll & R.A.M.C. This will be a great way to occupy these men, & give R.A.M.C. personnel for those own speciel work when required. Word	

WAR DIARY or INTELLIGENCE SUMMARY

Army Form C. 2118.

81st FIELD AMBULANCE,
27TH DIVISION,
EXPEDITIONARY FORCE.

Hour, Date, Place	Summary of Events and Information	Remarks and references to Appendices
Oct 8. 15 MORCOURT.	Have had complaints on apparent upon 3 of the men in the unit, testing the effect of a grease Vaseline & Mustard 1 – 16. It has been carried out over a period of 3 full days, under Trench Conditions. They were exempted from the usual Khaki demands, particularly between the toes (all & bowels amount evenly withheld in) Socks put on, & both lovely large fissures put on not too tight. The men rather their boots several times during the day. Observations. No thickening, capacity to march, not impaired, slight transient highness in one case, slight itchiness of feet in one case. cleanness of feet. complaint of no cost care. The wound being cork the cost element need not be taken as a result of the ointment. As one man complained of slight tenderness I suppose that the preparation's 8 Know 8% 2 appendices too strong. Rain report him sent to A.D.M.S. — finds Oct 9. 15 MORCOURT.	In state Emo

Army Form C. 2118.

WAR DIARY
or
INTELLIGENCE SUMMARY
(Erase heading not required.)

81ST FIELD AMBULANCE,
21TH DIVISION,
EXPEDITIONARY FORCE.

Instructions regarding War Diaries and Intelligence Summaries are contained in F. S. Regs, Part II. and the Staff Manual respectively. Title pages will be prepared in manuscript.

Hour, Date, Place	Summary of Events and Information	Remarks and references to Appendices

Oct – 10.15
MORCOURT

Arms & Vivres The Rob Staff, + reported on arrive (XII Corps)

Discussed where was the best place to cater for the early wounded of seven head, abdomen & chest cases.

(1) On a barge 4½ miles from the front

or

(2) At Corbie or Amiens 9½ + 18½ miles respectively.
CORBIE or AMIENS

My main point was The Abdominal Surgeons, if you could be supplied to be always at the barge, that the patient be alluded to them, & the set with them the Surgeon by very careful transport. There are very few men in my opinion who have had enough experience to deal with serious abdominal injuries and on their hands I forever even being sent to a C.C.S state since the supply of good surgeons is limited.

In the afternoon inspected Horse lines & collected to meet on the wounded area, and found that RMO's do not appear to pay sufficient zeal in advance time to arrange sanitary protection, & daily inspection of them wounded billets.

JW? B

WAR DIARY
or
INTELLIGENCE SUMMARY

(Erase heading not required.)

Army Form C. 2118.

31st FIELD AMBULANCE,
10th DIVISION
EXPEDITIONARY FORCE.

Hour, Date, Place	Summary of Events and Information	Remarks and references to Appendices
Oct 12.15.	Converted a house & barn into a Battn Stores at CERISY to take troops in that area. Am'ce personnel carried out the cleaning & cleaning etc. The Battns are to be run by "B" men of the Battalion. When litter & sqrn stores are supplied 30 or so Coys can be installed. Ford	
Oct 14.15	The personnel at the A.D. Statn CHUIGNES withdrawn & replaced by other personnel. "C" Sectn so that all bearers of "C" Sectn might become well acquainted with Adv. posn & method of clearing the front line. Ford	
Oct 15.15	Inspected with A.D.M.S. a large house at NARFUZEE MRANCOURT, with a view to taking it over for an Officers Rest Statn. It is a house vacated by owner the Henry Franculin hrs. left, but require many things to be bought in order to make it habitable & complete. Took on an Officer & made a list of necessary items, In the afternoon requisite & reconstructed the same & gave it over to A.D.M.S. for this afternoon for function fame. Sent a party of 4 men to clean the place, & act as orderlies to hand it. Ford	

Army Form C. 2118.

WAR DIARY
or
INTELLIGENCE SUMMARY

31ST FIELD AMBULANCE,
27TH DIVISION,
EXPEDITIONARY FORCE.

(Erase heading not required.)

Hour, Date, Place	Summary of Events and Information	Remarks and references to Appendices
Oct 18.15. MORCOURT.	Visited CORBIE to make an estimate of the prices offered for supplies to make suitable the proposed Officers Rest Stations, but the estimates have now come from S & "B" Sects. men for Retailers. This work very satisfactorily. A Sgt being in charge of an Officers Sub-factory. A Sgt being in charge of an Officers Supervisor. This letter about to the Field Ambulance. 1½ hours a day for 2 times.	
Oct 18.15 8. Am. MORCOURT.	Leave of absence for 5 days granted to me this day. Major Kay to be in charge.	Smith
Oct 22.15.	Driving to the ruins of the town all both coloured "B" men ordered to repair their respective units. 1 officers	
Oct 24.15	Park with Supply R.A. 1 Sgt & 5 men withdrawn to A.S.S. CHUIGNES. In anticipate of the Move.	good

Army Form C. 2118.

WAR DIARY
or
INTELLIGENCE SUMMARY

(Erase heading not required.)

81ST FIELD AMBULANCE,
27TH DIVISION.
EXPEDITIONARY FORCE.

Hour, Date, Place	Summary of Events and Information	Remarks and references to Appendices
Oct 25.15.	In the night of 24th–25th. The French took over the A-D-state at CHUIGNES, They men remain the main dressing state at MORCOURT. The Officers Rest State which was prepared at NARFUZEE has been given up on account of the move. It was nothing finished, nor occupied.	
Oct 26.15.	The Ambulance moved to MORCOURT 8.25 am 15 day by march route. Arrived at BOVES. Capt Green, 1 Sgt, 11 men stayed behind with 40 cases which were left in the Rest-State; 4 of these were sent to CCS the remainder 36 transport to 82nd Field Ambulance who had established a temporary Rest-State at FRESNEY. These men were later on moved by our main convoy. A few days. No 10 Motor Ambulance Convoy conveyed the patients. The Ambulance arrived at BOVES 4 P.M, & Bivouacked for the night. Horse Ambulances following. The Battalion in the Brigade. Motor Ambulances conveyed foot sore & there who were unable to march. These were made up mostly of "B" class men.	

Army Form C. 2118.

WAR DIARY
or
INTELLIGENCE SUMMARY

(Erase heading not required.)

21ST FIELD AMBULANCE,
27TH DIVISION,
EXPEDITIONARY FORCE.

Hour, Date, Place	Summary of Events and Information	Remarks and references to Appendices
Oct 27.15.	The Ambulance left Base Camp 5.30 am for March Route to MONTENOY. Halted for dinner. Reached MONTENOY 5 pm. Only the men of the unit fell out upon the march. I returned from leave, & joined the Ambulance at 6 pm at MONTENOY.	
Oct 28.15. BOUGAINVILLE	The Billets in MONTENOY being very inadequate for patients. Personnel, the Ambulance moved to BOUGAINVILLE 3 miles away from MONTENOY. Here is being established a temporary hospital in good Barns for the reception of sick from the 87th Brigade front.	
Oct 30.15. BOUGAINVILLE	Norms inspected the hospital & the 81st Brigade at their HQs. They were chiefly composed of men about 44 yrs old. Red. varicose veins, deformities, myalgia, and the men who had been classed "B". Then being disposed of by their respective units. Norms calling in Town Pay booth – hoped to find his half-norms men, were observing ? men who	

WAR DIARY or INTELLIGENCE SUMMARY

Army Form C. 2118.

81st FIELD AMBULANCE,
27TH DIVISION,
EXPEDITIONARY FORCE.

Hour, Date, Place	Summary of Events and Information	Remarks and references to Appendices
Oct. 30 · 15	Could not obtain a route campaign at the front, but who cannot do B war duties. There appears to have been many men sent up as draughts to Battalions, who should never have been found fit in the first instance. These have proved a great burden to us at times & when the Battalion move they invariably flood the Ambulance. Then again these men would do little or no good is a change on its an Physicals report in Trench warfare where the line is stationary, these men can be given suitable employment, but I think the folly of no one can say when a move will be made. Then again there is always a small percentage of recovering mild sick men who require light duty, who could be employed from Sanitary fatigues & non trench work, until they became thoroughly fit. These men could always move up if a push was on & all concerned. I feel sure the service would benefit by a thorough weeding out of unfit. (I mean the grade front-line).	

WAR DIARY
or
INTELLIGENCE SUMMARY

(Erase heading not required.)

Army Form C. 2118.

31ST FIELD AMBULANCE,
27TH DIVISION,
EXPEDITIONARY FORCE.

Hour, Date, Place	Summary of Events and Information	Remarks and references to Appendices
Oct 31./15.	Went to South Midland Casualty Clearing Station AMIENS to arrange the treatment of Dental & Eye Cases (at Rgn's request). Teeth Cases came a great deal of trouble. I am inclined to think that men without teeth, + with broken dentures (allowing the stores shoulder), would be that deprived I to the Base for Radical Treatment in the first instance, Kerby being a great deal of trouble time & expense. Radical treatment can't be carried out under existing conditions. Trench life to deserve. Men cannot stand boots. Trench life when they have with to marshals their feet, especially friends. Trench Feet. Had mentioned in the early part of the month that I would give a full report upon the absence made upon this condition; but since the Cases have been few, + the weather couldn't have good I cannot turn any conclusions. Undoubtedly the boots sent the Scene is inapt. I wonder if it be just possible to have some kind of asbestos lining	

1247 W 3299 200,000 (E) 8/14 J.B.C. & A.   Forms/C. 2118/11.

WAR DIARY or INTELLIGENCE SUMMARY

Army Form C. 2118.

81ST FIELD AMBULANCE,
27TH DIVISION,
BRITISH EXPEDITIONARY FORCE.

Hour, Date, Place	Summary of Events and Information	Remarks and references to Appendices
31.1.15	The boots & asbestos slippers & socks. I have in knapsack rather than can be manipulated into articles of clothing. Transport. There appears to be a general & equipment pertinent to general of transport to Italians 15 m. motor ambulance wagons an interpreter, a second / never made it impossible to take all the added equipment. I refer to Emergency Medicine Comforts weighing about 6 cuts. Oxygen Cylinder. Sprayers for Smoke Helmets. Carron Oil for Burns. Hypophosphate Soda. Seed Cake (GRO 419) Blankets 200 Pyjamas Suits 200 Woollen Red Socks 200 Bedroom Slippers 200. Reserve Smoke Helmets 400 to 6,500. Anti Frost Rub Grease reserve of 100 lb at the least (as at Tolken 20 lb to give a battalion men & this being done daily the estimate is small). Reserve dressings or motorcycle & carts with type of Karper. The Pannier are inadequate during the fighting. The call made upon us for dressings during the fighting we have to keep easing the stock up, to at least fighting we have to keep easing the stock up, to at least 6 to Fab 2 dressings over & above our establishment. GWR	

WAR DIARY
or
INTELLIGENCE SUMMARY

Army Form C. 2118.

31ST FIELD AMBULANCE,
27TH DIVISION,
EXPEDITIONARY FORCE.

Hour, Date, Place	Summary of Events and Information	Remarks and references to Appendices
Oct 31. 15.	The Reserve Kit of the R.A.M.C. (N.C.O's & men.) No provision is made by the War Office or Authorities for packs were with drawn & so it is laid down each man must have :— For provisions 1 shirt 1 vest 1 pr drawers 1 hold all complete, 1 towel, 1 comforter, 1 waterproof cape, soap & towel, & that the only way for them to carry them when on the move is to turn up their blanket & waterproof sheet (as there an intention in the Summary), & place them upon the clothes cart. The way laid down for them to carry their kit, I reply, it up in their great coat is made practical, not economical. In not wearing it is absurd, impossible. Then again when in a billet to leave one way of keeping his belongings together, some particular way of keeping things in. It was never on their own, to be with drawn of clothing things no fault of their own. The blanket cart is the unit: one is to be with drawn. This forces me into a difficulty which I think could be rectified by the issue of Valise Equipment to each man. When brought out from the Base they invariably bring along a Kit Bag, which is pardo' not on particular of the Valise Equipment.	

WAR DIARY
or
INTELLIGENCE SUMMARY

Army Form C. 2118.

81ST FIELD AMBULANCE,
27TH DIVISION
EXPEDITIONARY FORCE.

Hour, Date, Place	Summary of Events and Information	Remarks and references to Appendices
Oct 31.15. BOUGAINVILLE.	Transport:— I think a 30 cwt Motor lorry would be both economical & useful & meant to meet the nearer to transport. On several occasions at Ypres I found a Motor form to bring in sixty cases from the front. Since all the collecting had to be carried out between the hour of 9 & 3 Am. As many as 120 other ranks were brought into the dressing station by one night. Appointed Sends monthly State of Field Ambulance & Div Rest State = Continued.	J Smith Lt Colonel OC 81ST FIELD AMBULANCE, 27TH DIVISION, EXPEDITIONARY FORCE.

Army Form C. 2118.

31ST FIELD AMBULANCE,
27TH DIVISION,
EXPEDITIONARY FORCE.

WAR DIARY
or
INTELLIGENCE SUMMARY
(Erase heading not required.)

Hour, Date, Place	Summary of Events and Information	Remarks and references to Appendices

Oct 31. 15
BOUGAINVILLE
AMIENS

Monthly Statement of Sick and Wounded

Monthly Ret. Station from 1st to 27th October 1915

Remained		Admitted		Evacuated to C.C.S.		To C.C.S.		To O.H. Amb.		To duty		Remaining	
officers	o.Rks	officers	o.Rks	officers	o.Rks	officers	o.Rks	officers	o.Rks	officers	o.Rks	officers	o.Rks
2	87	15	587	1	277			11	384	1	59	6	505
	1		35						25		1		10
2	88	16	619	1	277			12	409	1	60	6	515

Brigade Sick from 27th to 31st October 1915.

Remained		Admitted		To C.C.S.		To C.C.S.		To duty		Remaining	
officers	o.Rks	officers	o.Rks	officers	o.Rks	officers	o.Rks	officers	o.Rks	officers	o.Rks
		2	50	2	11				10		29
			1		1						
	-	2	51	2	12				10		29

www.ingramcontent.com/pod-product-compliance
Lightning Source LLC
Chambersburg PA
CBHW081437160426
43193CB00013B/2306